T0358343

Cambridge Elements ≡

Elements in Beckett Studies
edited by
Dirk Van Hulle
University of Oxford
Mark Nixon
University of Reading

BECKETT AND DERRIDA

James Martell
Lyon College

CAMBRIDGE
UNIVERSITY PRESS

Shaftesbury Road, Cambridge CB2 8EA, United Kingdom

One Liberty Plaza, 20th Floor, New York, NY 10006, USA

477 Williamstown Road, Port Melbourne, VIC 3207, Australia

314–321, 3rd Floor, Plot 3, Splendor Forum, Jasola District Centre,
New Delhi – 110025, India

103 Penang Road, #05–06/07, Visioncrest Commercial, Singapore 238467

Cambridge University Press is part of Cambridge University Press & Assessment,
a department of the University of Cambridge.

We share the University's mission to contribute to society through the pursuit of
education, learning and research at the highest international levels of excellence.

www.cambridge.org
Information on this title: www.cambridge.org/9781009494366

DOI: 10.1017/9781009414364

First published 2024

A catalogue record for this publication is available from the British Library

ISBN 978-1-009-49436-6 Hardback
ISBN 978-1-009-41439-5 Paperback
ISSN 2632-0746 (online)
ISSN 2632-0738 (print)

Beckett and Derrida

Elements in Beckett Studies

DOI: 10.1017/9781009414364
First published online: December 2024

James Martell
Lyon College

Author for correspondence: James Martell, james.martell@lyon.edu

Abstract: Uncannily similar projects, Beckett's and Derrida's oeuvres have been linked by literary and philosophy scholars since the 1990s. Taking into consideration their shared historical and personal contexts as writers whose main language of expression was 'adopted' or 'imposed', this Element proposes a systematic reading of their main points of connection. Focusing on their engagement with the intricacies of beginnings and origins, on genetic grounds or surfaces analogous to the Platonic *khôra*, and on their similar critiques of the aporias of sovereignty, it exposes the reasons why multiple readers, like Coetzee, consider Derridean deconstruction a philosophical mirror of Beckett's literary achievements.

Keywords: Beckett, Derrida, modernism, sovereign, gender studies

ISBNs: 9781009494366 (HB), 9781009414395 (PB), 9781009414364 (OC)
ISSNs: 2632-0746 (online), 2632-0738 (print)

Contents

Introduction: 'I Only Have One Language; It Is Not Mine' or *Khôra* & The Sovereign

Ensconced within another quote, the only textual fragment of Samuel Beckett's work within Jacques Derrida's published corpus appears in *Clang*. It is a quote from *Molloy* where the homonymous character discusses how he named his mother:

> I called her Mag, when I had to call her something. And I called her Mag because for me, without my knowing why, the letter g abolished the syllable Ma, and as it were spat on it, better than any other letter would have done. And at the same time I satisfied a deep and doubtless unacknowledged need, the need to have a Ma, that is a mother, and to proclaim it, audibly. For before you say mag, you say ma, inevitably. And da, in my part of the world, means father. Besides, for me the question did not arise, at the period I'm working into now, I mean the question of whether to call her Ma, Mag or the Countess Caca, she having for countless years been as deaf as a post. (Beckett qtd in Derrida, 2021, 258b; Derrida, 1974, 322b)[1]

As this Element will show, it is appropriate that the literary and printed crossroads between these two authors takes place at a point where language, origin, and the maternal body coincide: the *khôratic* space. For it is the question of the literary, philosophical, writing, and/or written subject in front of the possibility of pronouncing its own origin that is at the heart of the modernist coincidence we can call 'Beckett and Derrida'. This significant coincidence has been differently remarked, in the past couple of decades, by scholars such as Steven Connor, Nicholas Royle, Shane Weller, Anthony Uhlmann, Daniel Katz, and even Coetzee, who, in 2006, called it a 'sympathetic vibration' (Coetzee, 2006, xiii). Asja Szafraniec's formidable comparative analysis of their oeuvres, *Derrida, Beckett, and the Event of Literature* (2007), is an obvious predecessor of – and interlocutor to – this Element. Its short epilogue connecting Derrida's and Beckett's desire for a writing beyond mastery was an initial point for this study. Nevertheless, even though it identifies some points of transaction, by focusing more on the philosophical reasons for Derrida's ultimate dismissal of Beckett as an exemplary 'literary event', it disregards its own insights as to the exact nature of their positive 'sympathetic vibration' (Coetzee, 2006, xiii). Such a sympathy lies at the aforementioned zone or *khôratic* space, foundational surface and abyss where language, origin, and the maternal body coincide. Its importance appears – beyond a shared focus on the feminine/maternal body and on its links to the mother tongue and the writer's self-created

---

[1] When considered relevant, I will give the pagination for the French text after the one from the English translation. Sometimes translations of texts other than Beckett's have been slightly modified to make them more literal.

style – in the ways it opens up the question of the (male) sovereign subject in the second half of the twentieth century. It is precisely this question that, from works like Richard Begam's *Samuel Beckett and the End of Modernity* (1996), up to Daniela Caselli's *Insufferable: Beckett, Gender and Sexuality* (2023) – passing through many other recent studies focused on posthumanism, embodiment, and the Anthropocene – points to Beckett's and Derrida's importance as critics of phallogocentrism as a schema founded on a supreme, total, and ultimate totalitarian subject; or, in other words, as deconstructors of the closure of Western metaphysics. While all the previous and contemporary works resonating the vibration between Beckett and Derrida examine or underscore indirectly an angle of their shared space of questioning, this Element proposes to focus directly on one of their and our most urgent ones: *khôra* or the m/other space of chorology as the unthought counterpart and ground of the sovereign modern subject and its logic of presence, power, and oppression, or of what Derrida (2000, 47) called *Bemächtigungstrieb* (from the German *bemächtigen*: to seize, possess, overpower). This chorology facing sovereignty and totalitarian drives is 'the *différantial* space that lies between modernism and antimodernism' described by Begam (1996, 7), the space where the modern subject confronts its genetic, metaphysic, sociopolitical, and literary aporias. It is also the 'breach' or the space 'prior to separation' that Trezise (1990, 28) saw in his Derridean reading of Beckett's impossibility to express, as a shared critique of the sovereignty of the phenomenological subject, or of the power to express by completely separating itself from the *khôratic* ground.[2] Therefore, in order to begin to listen to this sympathetic vibration in its complex *khôratic* space, and since *khôra* designates as well a region or land, we must look at the biographical and cultural context of both authors, while focusing on the questions of their languages, origins, and cultural identities.

Born in El Biar, in French Algeria, on 15 July 1930, Jacques 'Jackie' Derrida (named after Jackie Coogan, the child actor in Chaplin's 1921 *The Kid*) experienced the complicated upbringing of a Francophone Jewish Algerian 'Maghrébin', a French citizen of the colony of Algeria, growing up during World War II. Even before he was born, his origin had a complex linguistic and cultural dimension since the Derrida family had emigrated from Spain to France before 1870, when Algerian Jews received French nationality through the Crémieux Decree. Years later, Derrida would talk about the trauma of having lost his French nationality (even before he had visited France) as an Algerian

---

[2] While Trezise does not use the term '*khôra*' (since the homonymous essay by Derrida was not published until 1993, three years after *Into the Breach*), he does characterise the 'breach' as the *khôratic* space of a 'general economy', a 'pre-originary' involvement, or an 'immemorial dispossession' before the separation of the sovereign *cogito*.

Jew for two years during the occupation: 'I lost it for years without having another. You see, not the least one' (Derrida, 1998, 15). Having not learnt Hebrew, nor Berber or Arabic, let alone Spanish, but only the language of the coloniser, French, together with French mainland culture, Derrida described his complicated ownership of this given language with the statement: 'I only have one language; it is not mine' (Derrida, 1998, 1). While he characterised his relation to French in this way during a conference in April 1992 at Louisiana State University (in a text that would become *Le monolinguisme de l'autre*; 1996), he had already described such a pseudo-ownership of his own language, in 1989, precisely in the context of a question regarding Samuel Beckett.

When asked on this occasion by his interviewer, Derek Attridge, if he was planning to write on Beckett one day (since he had already mentioned Beckett in another interview; Kearny, 1995), Derrida answered by saying that, due to an extreme proximity with Beckett that he not only felt, but also wanted to feel ('to whom I would like to feel myself very close; but also too close'), it had been too difficult for him to write on Beckett's works (Derrida, 1992, 60). Then he added:

> Too hard also because he writes – in my language, in a language which is his up to a point, mine up to a point (for both of us it is a 'differently' foreign language) – texts which are both too close to me and too distant for me even to be able to 'respond' to them. (60)

By confessing this proximity and this shared complicated relation and pseudo-ownership of the French language, Derrida was referencing Beckett's own linguistic and cultural journey as an Irish-born, French-speaking writer, a descendant of a Huguenot family, who didn't speak the 'national language' of his country of birth,[3] yet could speak Italian and German, and chose French apparently not out of an attempt to master a foreign culture (or to restore a lost familial language), but instead as a paradoxical effort to reduce, if not to lose, mastery over his own writerly activity. Years before he adopted French as his main writerly language after the war, in his 1929 contribution to *Our Exagmination Round His Factification for Incamination of Work in Progress* (the *transition* adjacent collective volume in support of Joyce's *Work in Progress*, soon to be titled *Finnegans Wake*), Beckett had already expressed a dissatisfaction with the English language and its abstractions: 'Mr Joyce has desophisticated language. And it is worth remarking that no language is so sophisticated as English. It is abstracted to death' (Beckett, 1984a, 28). The question, at this point, for Beckett, seemed to be how to continue Joyce's labour of 'desophistication' but without being engulfed by

---

[3] As Alan Graham describes it, 'the perceived nexus between language and identity' was 'one of the most – if not *the* most – politically charged issues in the Ireland of Beckett's youth' (Graham, 2021, 58).

it – a fear expressed at the beginning of the same essay: 'And now here I am, with my handful of abstractions [. . .] and the prospect of self-extension in the world of Mr Joyce's *Work in Progress*' (19).[4] In a similar way as Derrida would express it decades later in the only book of his that inhabited Beckett's personal library, *Ulysse gramophone* (1987), Beckett knew that Joyce's experiment – as valid and necessary as it had been – had gone as far as possible not in spite of but rather because of its mastery and voraciousness, namely its *bemächtigen*. As he expressed it to James Knowlson, two years after *Ulysse gramophone* had come out:

> I realised that Joyce had gone as far as one could in the direction of knowing more, [being] in control of one's material. He was always adding to it; you only have to look at his proofs to see that. I realised that my own way was in impoverishment, in lack of knowledge and in taking away, in subtracting rather than in adding. (Knowlson, 1996, 319)

This notion of Joyce's project as a literary enterprise of 'addition' resonates thus with Derrida's description of Joyce's oeuvre, in *Ulysse gramophone*, as a 'literature of burden [*somme*] as one speaks of a "beast of burden", literature of summons [*sommation*], moment of the debt' (Derrida, 2013, 69; Derrida, 1987b, 119). As a consequence, the opposite experiment, a literary exercise like Beckett's, based on impoverishment, lack of knowledge, and taking away, could be called – as Derrida agreed, answering to Attridge – essentially 'deconstructive', if not 'deconstruction' itself. What is more, Beckett's chosen adoption of French could also be seen as a way to, through distancing, deconstruct by defamiliarisation his own language and cultural identity (see Dennis, 2019). As a matter of fact, both Beckett and Derrida saw their writerly projects – and, with them, the future of literature and/or philosophy – not in addition, incorporation, comprehensiveness, and totalities. Instead, they saw them in subtraction, reduction, or deconstruction of the encyclopaedic edifices and the 'metaphysical assumptions behind Western thought' (Coetzee, 2006, xiii), literature, and philosophy. The reasons why they both saw this need of subtraction and de-structuration lie not only in their personal experiences, but also in the cultural context they shared: World War II and its aftermaths in Europe and beyond. In other words, their aesthetic, literary, and philosophical enterprises were not only determined by and directed against a purely literary-philosophical tradition. They were also marked by their historical and cultural circumstances as 'immigrant' authors who adopted French as their language (one after a colonial imposition, the other as a literary and experiential choice), while they were immersed in the philosophical but also experiential questions and aporias of the

---

[4] This is a fear or even resentment in front of Joyce's omnivorous project described well by Derrida in 'Two Words for Joyce' (Derrida, 2013, 24). See also Katz (1999, 127).

French, European, and Western traditions that reached a crisis, and finally their nadir, with the Holocaust (see Salisbury, 2015, 9).

Seen in this context, Beckett's statements in the famous German letter to Axel Kaun of 1937 regarding, first English, and then language in general, reveal a preoccupation not only with his own developing aesthetic but also with an outdated tradition in need of revision, if not destruction. Or, as Beckett expressed it: 'it does not suffice if the game loses some of its sacred solemnity. It should stop' (Beckett, 2009, 520). Accordingly, what at first seems an artistic necessity, or even the personal impossibility to do something in an official, formal, or normal way, quickly reveals itself as an ethical imperative for any contemporary writer, a command to misuse language, until what sustains or lies below it – that is to say, its foundations or reason – comes through:

> It is indeed getting more and more difficult, even pointless, for me to write in *formal* [*offizielles*] English. And more and more my language appears to me like a veil which one has to tear apart in order to get to those things (or the nothingness) lying behind it. *Grammar and style*! To me they seem to have become as irrelevant as a Biedermeier bathing suit or the imperturbability [*Unerschüttlichkeit*] of a gentleman. A mask [*Larve*]. It is to be hoped the time will come, thank God, in some circles it already has, when language is best used where it is most efficiently abused. Since we cannot dismiss it all at once, at least we do not want to leave anything undone that may contribute to its disrepute. To drill one hole after another into it until that which lurks behind, be it something or nothing, starts seeping through – I cannot imagine a higher goal for today's writer. (Beckett, 2009, 513–14, 518; my emphasis)

By linking grammar and style with a Biedermeier swimsuit and with the imperturbability of a gentleman, Beckett is remarking here not only the conditions of officialness and propriety demanded by the cultural and literary traditions of the nineteenth and twentieth centuries. He is also underlining the sphere of 'authenticity' as that which is 'naturally' dictated by cultural and, more significantly, biological origins (for example, it is *natural* for a writer to write in his own mother tongue, English). While this comment on contemporary culture could be seen as a Beckettian instantiation of the critique of the inauthenticity of being that Heidegger called *das Man* ('the "they"') (see Heidegger, 2008), Beckett's questioning of the modern subject will go further, since it will seek to erode not only authentic normality and officialness, but also the notion of authenticity or the proper itself in all spheres (see Katz, 1999, no. 6, 198).

As we know, such an examination of the authentic, the proper, and the natural, together with the concomitant dangers of their intertwining in the desire for full, sovereign presence and meaning, characterises Derrida's work from the start. Heidegger's *Destruktion* of metaphysics was a model (in conjunction with other problematics, like the nature of the sign in Husserlian phenomenology, or the notion of origin in Rousseau) for Derrida's initial conception of deconstruction, as well as a constant reference in all of his subsequent work. Thus, given Derrida's continuous engagement with Heidegger's oeuvre, and Beckett's relation with the main champion of Heidegger in France during the war years, Jean Beaufret, and his mingling with the intellectual circles of *Les Temps modernes* where Heidegger's work was discussed, I agree with Rodney Sharkey's perception of Heidegger's work as a main connector between Beckett's and Derrida's oeuvres – especially when conceived as deconstructive struggles against fascism and the worst of Western culture (Sharkey, 2010, 411).

Derrida's philosophical and writerly investigation of this essential complicity between the desire for presence and for the authentic went through different stages and questions throughout his life. As we will see, these different stages have thematic and formal correspondences with Beckett's own developments, remarking thus different facets of their 'sympathetic vibration'. If their biggest coincidence is that, as Szafraniec puts it, they 'both deconstruct the self-present human subject' and 'institute the delay of self-presence as the source of the authorial "I"' (Szafraniec, 2007, 118), such an achievement is not a simple action, performed conceptually only once. In other words, this shared deconstruction and affirmation of deferral and difference involves a multiplicity of movements of decentring, deflection, and analysis, affecting not only the subject and its purported sovereignty, but also our languages, conceptions of origin, and the bodies through and in which we are born, live, speak, and die. Further, the 'sympathetic vibration' of their deconstruction affects not only the private, subjective experience of the writer and reader. By questioning some of the basic tenets of Western philosophy and thought (the teleology of discourse and life, the limits of the sovereign subject, the world, history, and of any delimited totality), their projects also examine and question – in different yet resonating performative manners – our collective ways of being, as well as the assumed naturally given conditions of thought, art, and expression. It is this multifaceted complexity of their critiques of Western cultures that drives the different angles of this Element, centred nevertheless on the encounter in the two oeuvres between the overpowering sovereign and the *khôratic* space where it/he rises and dies.

Given the complex intertwining of the questions of subject, language, and origin in their work, it is unsurprising that both Beckett and Derrida placed the mothers and the question of maternity and birth at the centre of their projects. As proof of this centrality, there is not only Beckett's famous affirmation to MacGreevy in 1937 – same year as the letter to Axel Kaun – saying: 'I am what her savage loving has made me' (Beckett, 2009, 552), or even Geoffrey Thompson's statement that the 'key to understanding Beckett [. . .] was to be found in his relationship with his mother' (qtd in Knowlson, 1996, 172). More importantly, figures of May Beckett, as well as of other semi-anonymous mothers, constantly haunt Beckett's corpus, confirming his statement, from 1948 to Georges Duthuit, that, for his life and for his work, he might need no other eyes but his mother's:

> I keep watching my mother's eyes, never so blue, so stupefied, so heart-rending, eyes of an endless childhood, that of old age. Let us get there rather earlier, while there are still refusals we can make. I think these are the first eyes that I have seen. I have no wish to see any others, I have all I need for loving and weeping. I know now what is going to close, and open inside me, but without seeing anything, there is no more seeing. (Beckett, 2011, 92)

In the case of Derrida, as he expressed it in the most literary and personal text of his oeuvre, 'Circumfession', not only the figure of his mother, but also the temporal coincidence between her dying and his writing of this confessional text, becomes central. Linking himself to Saint Augustine, who also wrote through the mourning of his own mother (and a copy of whose *Confessions* remained in Beckett's library until the end), Derrida also considers the possibility, like Beckett, that his eyes – also weeping – could amalgamate with his mother's, and thus allow for a substitution of him for her, similar to Molloy's:[5]

> that child whom the grown-ups amused themselves by making cry for nothing, who was always to weep over himself with the tears of his mother: 'I'm sorry for myself', 'I make myself unhappy', 'I'm crying for myself', 'I'm crying over myself' – but like another, another wept over by another weeper, *I weep from my mother over the child whose substitute I am.* (Derrida and Bennington, 1993, 118–19; my emphasis)

Thus, with their writerly and deconstructive projects essentially linked to their own mothers, births, and notions of maternity, it is neither a coincidence nor just anecdotal evidence that Beckett's most important writerly 'revelation' – what will determine his own path and literary idiom of subtraction against Joyce's masterwork of addition – happened at his dying mother's room: 'Krapp's vision was on the pier at Dún Laoghaire; mine was in my mother's room. Make that clear once and for all' (qtd in Knowlson, 1996, 319).

If, as Jean-Michel Rabaté writes in *Beckett and Sade*, the biggest dream for an artist is to give birth to themselves, becoming their own creator (Rabaté, 2020, 40), or, as Angela Moorjani exclaims – following Ehrenzweig – 'the birthing process is the central myth of artistic creation' (Moorjani, 1982, 138), this dream, as Derrida pointed out in 'La veilleuse' (Derrida, 2013, 100), does not

---

[5] For a consideration of Beckett's relation to Augustinian 'autography', see H. Porter Abbott (1996).

arise without the realisation of its annihilating consequence: the effacing not only of the artist's first birth, but with it, also of their mother, and potentially, of maternity itself. This violent consequence points out to a complication already present in the modern notion of the sovereign subject, namely if the subject must be conceived as sovereign (absolutely independent, self-sufficient, and so on), how much of *his* sovereignty (since we have not yet finished deconstructing the links between the universal and the masculine) is realised, or comes to be, at the expense of that against which he affirms itself, or of that against which he defines his 'purity' or 'totality'?[6] What is more, how much of this sovereignty is constantly threatened by the realisation of its delusive character, given that, ultimately, in modernity, no absolute divide, limit, or separation – as Trezise shows – is possible between subjects, objects, their environments, and all the interstices, thresholds, and abysses in between; or, to utilise a cherished figure and simile in Beckett's work, since, ultimately, there is no absolute divide between Dives and Lazarus, or 'from the unseen to the seen' (Beckett, 2006a, 167)?[7]

As we can expect, such questions of sovereignty and dreams of purity bring us back to the shared political and historical context of Beckett and Derrida. As the growing recent scholarship on the political and historical dimensions of Beckett's works,[8] together with the increasing interest on what Beckett's oeuvre can tell us about gender and ecocriticism questions[9] show, far from being an abstract modernist instantiation of 'l'art pour l'art', Beckett's literature is deeply engaged with modernity, modern history and society, and, particularly, with their aporias. Similarly, even if Derrida's early works were originally seen as 'metaphysical', his purportedly 'ethical turn' in the 1980s and 1990s did not mark a new opening to ethics and moral questions. When read carefully, we can see since the beginning a Derridean preoccupation with philosophical questions of real ethical consequences: questions of purity, of secondariness, of otherness, of sexual difference, and so on. Thus, the 'sympathetic vibration' or shared deconstructive perspectives of Beckett's and Derrida's writings lie precisely in

---

[6] For an analysis of this modernist tendency to totalising and totalitarianism, see my 'Modernism's Totalities' (Martell, 2024b).

[7] For a Merleau-Pontian reading of this erasure of the divide between characters and their environment, see Amanda Dennis (2021).

[8] Will Davies and Helen Bailey do an extraordinary tally of what they call 'The Political Turn' in Beckett studies in their introduction to *Beckett and Politics* (2021).

[9] To mention just a few examples: the recent conferences 'Samuel Beckett and the Anthropocene' (Trinity College, 2020), 'Samuel Beckett and Nature' (Lyon College, 2022), 'Lost Bodies: Beckett, Gender, and Sexuality' (Trinity College Dublin, 2022), 'Beckett's Environments' (2023); the *SBT/A* special issues 'Samuel Beckett and the Nonhuman' (2020) and 'Stepping down into the sexpit: Sex and Gender in Samuel Beckett's Work' (2022); three Elements in this series: McMullan's *Beckett's Intermedial Ecosystems*, Byron's *Samuel Beckett's Geological Imagination*, and Caselli's *Insufferable: Beckett, Gender and Sexuality*; Eleanor Green's upcoming project 'Queer Beckett', and so on.

a series of similar stylistic and thematic strategies whereby thinking realises the limits and frames of the Western tradition that reached a critical point in the middle of the twentieth century. Consequently, if the personal, contextual, and historical coincidences between the two authors can reveal us something, it is precisely how the question of the person or subject – as it was understood through our modern tradition and its male Cartesian avatars – cannot be thoroughly thought without an extreme experiential questioning of the philosophical and literary frames of said tradition. Ultimately, it is precisely such an experiential and performative critical strategy that accounts for the difficulty of both Beckett's and Derrida's works, and for their necessity.

1 General Writing

Multiple Beginnings

'Where to begin?' This common narratological question can highlight not only the particularity of the difference and sameness between the beginning of the two versions of Beckett's *L'innommable/The Unnamable*, where the second and third questions are inverted, while the first one – the topological – remains the same: '*Où maintenant?* Quand maintenant? Qui maintenant?' / '*Where now*? Who now? When now?' (Beckett, 1992, 7; Beckett, 2006b, 285; my emphasis). It also highlights a basic philosophical problem, the question of place and space in relation to beginning; or, in other words, the question of the ground as the ultimate foundation of thought and being. This is a question that is extremely significant for German philosophy, from Meister Eckhard, through the Idealists (Fichte, Hegel, but particularly Schelling), up to Heidegger, and through them, for both Beckett and Derrida. As we will see, it is through the ground's paradoxical conjunction of a particular materiality and a transcendental dimension as both foundation and reason (*Grund*) that Derrida and Beckett would utilise it in their own interrogations of our Western literary and philosophical tradition.

As Daniella Caselli shows in *Beckett's Dantes*, such a question of the ground as origin was not only fundamental (or '*grundlegend*') to *The Unnamable*, but also to a later text like *How It Is*: 'From the very first paragraph the text questions notions of origin, beginning, and presence, as the French title does by punning on the homophony between "comment c'est" and "commencer"' (Caselli, 2005, 149). Amanda Dennis explores how 'aporia in *The Unnamable* persists – literally – in the ground of this world so as to bring about its reconfiguration' (Dennis, 2021, 120). As I tried to show elsewhere (Martell, 2013), the imbrication, in *How It Is*, between the ultimate ontological (comment c'est: 'how it *is*') and genealogical ('*commencer*': 'to begin') questions mirrors the conundrum of Hegel at the beginning of *The Phenomenology of Spirit*, as Derrida analysed it in *La dissémination*. As Derrida points out, the contradiction between Hegel's criticism of the inanity of prologues and introductions in philosophy, and his own inclusion of a preface (*Vorrede*) and an introduction (*Einleitung*) in *The Phenomenology of Spirit*, bespeak of the chronological and topological problem of a philosophical work that pretends to tell the story of both, a particular consciousness and the history of all consciousnesses (Spirit), from the point of view of their already fulfilled end. While such a fold in the teleology of a book appeared already in Proust's *A la recherche du temps perdu* (where, at the end, we read the main character's initial decision to finally begin writing the book that we are just about to finish), it is not until Beckett that we see a consistent reflection on this aporia of a desire to write that which must already be finished before we start.[10] Since most modern novels tell of the development of a subject (*Bildung*), this is the desire to write not only a text (that is already finished and published), but also the subject of writing itself. In other words, as Porter Abbott showed, and paraphrasing a Lacanian formulation, we could say that this writerly desire is the desire of 'autography', namely the desire to write both the subject of writing (enunciation) and the written-subject (of the *énoncé*) from a place where they both have already been written. On the other hand, in this impossibility to decide the beginning, we could say, following Porter Abbott, that both writing and written self are ultimately '"unborn". Not going anywhere, they remain bound within that original womb in which the text in effect delivers itself' (Abbott, 1996, 11); that is to say, within *khôra*.

Such an aporia within the desire to write what must already have been written – and thus to become the subject that must have already been born or written for this becoming to begin – is not limited, in Beckett corpus, to *The Unnamable* and *How It Is*.[11] Furthermore, such a circularity appears not only in singular works like *Molloy*, with its second part, Moran's narration, negating its own beginning through a sweeping epanorthosis ('It is midnight. The rain is beating on the windows. It was no midnight. It was not raining'; Beckett, 2006b, 170), or in the semi-cyclical structure of plays like *Waiting for Godot*, *Not I*, *Play*, and even *Endgame*, where we expect for the end to just open up into a new, barely altered repetition of the beginning – or as Hamm says 'The end is in the beginning and yet you go on' (Beckett, 2006c, 141).[12] As Beckett scholars know well, the repetition of beginnings happens not only in these concrete works, but it also takes place among them, with 'each successive character in the series being conceived of as

---

[10] Anna McMullan also underscores this parallel Beckett/Proust (McMullan, 2021, 27).

[11] For a consideration of this aporia in terms of the constituted subject of expression in Derrida and Beckett, see Trezise (1990).

[12] Similarly, as Laura Salisbury suggests, the inaugural 'nothing to be done' of Estragon in *Waiting for Godot* already marks that 'the beginning is already the end; the "last moment" [...] has already been reached' (Salisbury, 2015, 37).

a repetition and a reimagination at the same time' (Connor, 2007, 57). That is to say, not only characters from earlier books make continuous appearances in following works (like Watt in *Mercier and Camier*, or Belacqua in *Molloy* and *Company*, or even Hamm and Clov as later incarnations of Vladimir and Estragon) (see Bair, 1978, 468), but also the structure and themes themselves in Beckett's oeuvre enact a constant rebirth and refashioning of previous texts (Connor, 2007, 2). As Angela Moorjani describes it, 'the stratified structure is repeated not only within each text, but from one to the other' (Moorjani, 1982, 53). Such a perpetual repetition of the beginning at and *as* the end is what is expressed in birthing incipits like 'Birth was the death of him' and *Not I*'s 'out ... out, into this world', significantly uttered by a female voice supposed to be old, ancient, or even spectrally immortal like *khôra*. Needless to say, the gendering of such voices and characters is extremely important, especially when examined through Derrida's own investigation into the ontological and genealogical conundrums of sexual difference and of modernist writers' denial of their maternal birth, through what he called 'the logic of obsequence' (a neologism composed of the French terms 'obsèques' [funeral service] and 'sequence'), and 'the logic of pregnancy'. According to the first one, which Derrida developed in *Clang* through a conjoined reading of Jean Genet's novels and Hegel's philosophy, the mother will not only always precede the writer, but will also always follow him:

> I am [*suis*] (following) the mother. The text. The mother is behind [*derrière*] – all that I follow, am, do, seem – the mother follows. Because she follows absolutely, she always survives – future that will never have been presentable – what she will have engendered, attending, impassive, fascinating and provocative; the interring of that whose death she foresaw. The logic of obsequence. (Derrida, 2021, 34; Derrida, 1974, 134b)

The second logic appears in *The Post Card*, and it implies that anything that one can write, even if it denies or questions one's own birth and consequently one's own mother and potentially all of maternity, would have already been included within the mother:

> This is what I call in English the logic of *pregnancy* and in French the foreclosure of the name of the mother. In other words, you are all born, don't forget, and you can write only against your mother who bore within her, along with you, what she has borne you to write against her, your writing with which she would be pregnant. And full, you will never get out of it. (Derrida, 1987a, 150)

Between Husserl and Joyce: Beckett's Undeconstructible Idiom

In his introduction to his translation of Husserl's *Origin of Geometry*, Derrida pits Husserl's phenomenological project against Joyce's literary endeavour as two attempts to test, by sovereign thinkers, the extreme possibilities of language in a final apprehension of the ultimate truth of the world and the self (see Martell, 2020, 106). For Derrida, Joyce's project tries to express a semantic and experiential totality through generalised equivocity, while Husserl's attempts the same task but through pure univocity.

When, two decades later, Derrida saw the closest resonance of his own project in neither Joyce's nor Husserl's project, but in Beckett's, it also was in relation to certain extreme possibilities of language. But these were not any more the possibilities of full capture or total comprehension either in an extreme plurivocality or through a full transparency. They were, rather, the extremity of the limits of language itself in general, and particularly of philosophical language. Hence, the first time Derrida mentioned Beckett in an interview – together with Bataille and Blanchot – was in the context of literary texts that make the limits of our logical concepts, and of language itself 'tremble' (qtd in Kearney, 1995, 162). As we have seen, the second and – as far as we know – last time, he gave as a reason for his not having yet written anything particular on Beckett's oeuvre, a desired proximity between their languages, while describing and concurring with the necessity of the operations that Beckett performed on language, which – according to Derrida – must nevertheless remain idiomatic. Noticing this agreement, Derek Attridge asked Derrida if one could say then that Beckett's writing was 'already so "deconstructive", or "auto-deconstructive", that there is not much left to do' (Derrida, 1992, 61). Derrida acquiesced, explaining that a certain nihilism that is both interior and beyond metaphysics is also simultaneously and at competition within Beckett's oeuvre. This self-contradicting nihilism is something Derrida had expressed in other instances, especially when considering the personal or autographic character of his work. For example, at the end of Safaa Fathy's film *D'ailleurs, Derrida*, he exclaims – as a statement whose addressee would have been his mother, again, as in 'Circumfession':

> I'd have liked to announce to G, my mother, who since forever does not hear me anymore, that which one must know before dying, to wit, that not only I do not know anybody, I have never met anybody, I have never had the idea throughout the history of humanity of anybody [. . .] who has been happier than me, and lucky, euphoric. It is a priori true, isn't it? Drunk on uninterrupted enjoyment. But that, if I remained the counter-example of myself, likewise constantly sad, denied, destitute, disappointed, impatient, jealous, desperate, and that if, finally, the two certainties do not exclude each other, then I ignore how to risk the least phrase without letting drop to the ground in silence, to the ground its lexicon, to the ground its grammar and its geology (*géologique*), how to say other thing than an interest just as passionate as disillusioned for those things, language, literature, philosophy, another thing that the impossibility to still say, like I do here, 'myself, I sign'. (My translation).

This necessary contradictory affirmation of both maximum, continuous joy and an equal degree of sadness and destitution as the requisite to risk any expression – and any signing self – shows Derrida's own self-deconstruction as the condition of possibility of his signature. In the same interview with Attridge, Derrida sees Beckett's signature – the one he considers himself incapable of responding to because of its proximity – as composed of a similar logic of contradictory remains:

> The composition, the rhetoric, the construction and the rhythm of his works, even the ones that seem the most 'decomposed', that's what 'remains' at bottom the most 'interesting', that's the oeuvre, that's the signature, this remainder which remains when the thematics is exhausted. (Derrida, 1992, 61)

Thus, if Beckett's oeuvre is a quintessential example of a literary work that makes the limits of logic and of our 'language tremble' (Derrida qtd in Kearney, 1995, 162), this function is dependent on an idiomatic affirmation of an irresolvable tension within the writing subject. Such a tension is what Shane Weller called Beckett's 'resistance of nihilism' (Weller, 2005, 24; my emphasis), emphasising the double genitive, and thus the reversible struggle of Beckett or Derrida, against themselves.[13] What is more, while – Derrida concedes – there are idioms in Joyce, Husserl, or Blanchot and Bataille, these idioms can still be separated or divided enough to discuss them and thus to respond to their authors. In the case of Beckett – like with Derrida's – the idiom must be undeconstructable since it is, ultimately, auto-deconstruction itself.

But how is this auto-deconstructability of Beckett's idiom constituted? In other words, what does it mean that an idiom is defined by its own deconstruction? If, according to Derrida, Beckett's undesconstructible (as an auto- or self-deconstructive) idiom inhabits the same language as his own, what is the form of its writerly becoming, its 'autography' as Porter Abbott rightly calls it, or its grammatology? According to Derrida, from the Belacqua of *Dream of Fair to Middling Women*, to the figures in *Worstward Ho* and *What Where*, what constitutes the unity of Beckett's idiom would lie in a purportedly auto-deconstructive structural movement beyond its thematics. Now, since Derrida's own project – at least at the beginning – can be seen as the development of a general notion of writing that questioned the primacy of the voice as the quintessential incarnation of full presence, Beckett's own self-deconstructive work must perform a similar critique, developed too through a writing over the self-present voice, or through what we could term – playing on Derrida's own notion of grammatology – a certain 'grammatologophony'. Now, as mentioned

---

[13] Derrida's last interview, for *Le Monde* (18 August 2004), titled 'I am at war with myself', emphasises the centrality of such a struggle for his philosophy.

earlier, such an act of writing incorporating the aporias of both the voice and the written mark is not unrelated to the way Porter Abbott distinguished Beckett's writing project as 'autography' in contrast to traditional 'autobiography', the former denoting all self-writing, the latter the narrative form that encompasses a life's story. What is more, Abbott's agreement with Derrida's insight – culled from the Derek Attridge interview – that what constitutes the irreducibility of Beckett's work is not the thematics but rather the composition, or what Abbott calls his 'autographical music' (Abbott, 1996, 62), points too to Derrida's insistence on the link between writing, the signature, and the writerly subject's mortality – especially as he developed them in 'Signature Event Context'.[14] For our purposes, it is not coincidental that it is in his chapter on *Krapp's Last Tape* where Abbott underscores the closest links – in his view – between Beckett's and Derrida's conceptions of their work, that is to say, in the autographical text '[w]here Krapp expels, Beckett mothers' (65); or, in other words, where the genetic and mortal separation between text, son, or crap-oeuvre and voice, mother, or author-subject is at stake.

Derrida's main literary example of writing's primacy over voice in *Voice and Phenomenon*, the voice of Poe's M. Valdemar saying 'I am dead', exemplifies a common situation for the majority of Beckett's grammatologophonic characters: the undecidability not only of their living/dead conditions, but also of the present/absent ontological character of their voices.[15] In other words, Beckett's grammatologophony is displayed in purgatorial landscapes and through ghostly characters not only because of their liminal after-death situation, but also because such a situation exemplifies the ontological status of any writing, tracing, or recording of a voice, where '"death", or the possibility of the "death" of the addressee [is] inscribed in the structure of the mark [...] and the value or effect of transcendentality is linked necessarily to the possibility of writing and of "death"' (Derrida, 1982, 316). What is more, for the primacy of the trace, writing, or recording over the – desire for the – living voice to be fully remarked, Beckett has the absent voice narcissistically doubled into a purportedly present one, underscoring the unerasable alterity within the sameness of the character. Thus, in an early work like *Watt*, the grammatologophonetic dimension of the characters and their discourse is layered in a variety of systems of inscription, from the aural, exemplified by the voice

---

[14] In Derrida's own autography there is an insistence on rhythm as well. See *La dissemination* and *Glas*, among other texts.

[15] So many Beckettian figures speak, like M. Valdemar, from the afterlife. What is more, as Caselli has rightly shown, Beckett's own incorporation of many Dantes is due, in a great part, to the undecidable purgatorial state of Dante's own figures. Steven Connor had already seen this Poesque coincidence in Beckett (Connor, 2007, n. 2, 224–5), but he linked it to Barthes, instead of to Derrida.

that Watt hears and its duplication in Watt's own voice telling the story to Sam, to the written texts of Sam, the narrator, the implicit author of the story, and, ultimately, Beckett himself. Such a layered system of transmission – taken to its extreme in the undefinable source of the quoted text/voice that is *How It Is* – demonstrates performatively the inherent alterity within identity. Ultimately, it is this alterity within sameness that allows Beckett to question so many presuppositions of Western culture, or what Derrida calls phallogocentrism, as recent important works in Beckett studies show, where the alterity of embodiment (Dennis, 2021), of technology and nature (Maude, 2011), of human and animal thought (Boulter, 2020; Rabaté, 2016), and of 'comic' matter (Salisbury, 2015) is unassimilable – and unerasable – by the sameness of presence.

Thus, it makes sense that Beckett's most intimate or idiomatic writerly confession should take place in a work like *Krapp's Last Tape*, where the main character's foil are the recordings of his own self. Nevertheless, the reflexivity between recorded voice and writing in the context of a doubling of the self takes place in an even more literal sense twenty years later in *Ohio Impromptu*, where an unspoken idiom – 'the unspoken words [. . .] the dear name' (Beckett, 2006c, 474–5) – gets insinuated in the middle of the doubled (if not tripled or more) reflection between Reader, Listener, the characters in the worn volume of the story, and those within the material book on the table on set.[16] As we know, such a doubling of the recorded/written over the presently spoken is embodied also in plays like *Rockaby* and *Footfalls*. In this latter one, the embodiment of the voice in an older woman points not only to May Beckett, but also to Derrida's logic of obsequence, namely, to the ur-maternal voice surviving and commenting on Beckett's text and whole oeuvre, as when M remarks 'Old Mrs. Winter, *whom the reader will remember*' (Beckett, 2006c, 430; my emphasis).

If these narcissistic doublings are a mark of Beckett's idiomatic self-deconstruction, it is also because, as Derrida recognised it, the aporias of narcissism are 'the explicit theme of deconstruction' (Derrida, 2006b, 122). In a similar way, Beckett's early choice of Belacqua as his writerly avatar sets up, through Belacqua's etymology of 'beautiful water', his fiction as a narcissistic mirror. However, if among all the infinite repetitions and reflections in Beckett's corpus, there is always an unspoken idiom like 'the dear name' (Beckett, 2006c, 475), 'the true words at last' (Beckett qtd in Knowlson, 1996, 601), or the looked-for word of the final poem 'What is the word', it is because literature, as Derrida remarked, has a taste for the secret. This secret is what Angela Moorjani

---

[16] This n+ reflection is what Moorjani describes as 'infinite reduplication' in Beckett (Moorjani, 1982, 22).

described, among all the discourses and narratives in *Watt*, 'linked to the archeology of Western thought', as 'the unknowable, unreachable, unnamable within Watt' (Moorjani, 1982, 37). As the same novel shows, such a secret or hidden idiom sometimes takes the shape, in our traditions, of a lost centre.

Circles and Centres

There is a familiar topological, geometric, and kinetic structure in Beckett from the early works up to the last ones. The best portrait of it is given in *Watt*'s painting in Erskine's room, describing the indeterminate search of a centre for a or its circle. But while it insistently appears as an obsession with the centre in texts like *Mal vul mal dit* (with the hut 'At the inexistent centre of a formless space'; Beckett, 2006d, 451) and *Endgame* (with Hamm's obsession to be put back in the exact centre of the room after his turns around the world), its most significant visual configurations appears nearly thirty years after *Watt*, in *Quad I* and *II*. The significance of the centre in these two visual and spatial allegories can be understood by the word that Beckett gave to it when discussing the *Quad* works in German (see Hans Hiebel, 1995): the *Abgrund* (Abyss). Such use of the German term underlines Beckett's understanding and preoccupation with the aforementioned notion of *Grund* as reason or foundation in German philosophy. Sharing the same German Idealism's inheritance as Beckett, Derrida developed too, from the beginning of his career, the aporias of the ontological notion of centre as reason (*Grund*) and abyss (*Abgrund*), with essays like 'Structure, Sign, and Play in the Discourse of the Human Sciences' and 'Ellipsis' from *Writing and Difference* (1967), and later, in *Rogues* (2003). Presaging *Quad*'s characters' terrorised avoidance of the centre, and remarking on structuralism's paradoxical need for a centre, he wrote in the first essay: 'Why would one mourn for the center? Is not the center, the absence of play and difference, another name for death? The death which reassures and appeases, but also, with its hole, creates anguish and puts at stake?' (Derrida, 1978, 374).

In *Ulysse gramophone*, Derrida showed how Joyce's *Ulysses* develops the abysmal and comedic aporias of both the Ulyssean return to self and the 'Ulyssean circle of the encyclopedia' (Derrida, 2013, 60), two purportedly self-enclosing and self-returning circles that always end up thwarted by the inherent alterity of their desire for closure. While, in *Writing and Difference* he focused on the aporetic desire of the circle and centre of a structure or system as a critique of structuralism – and as part of his development of a new notion of 'writing' vis-à-vis 'the age of the book' – in *Rogues*, he went back to the circle and centre, but this time, focusing on how they exemplify the presuppositions of democracy as a closed circle of sovereign subjects, in other words, of subjects capable to turn and return to themselves.

> The turn, the turn around the self – and the turn is always the possibility of turning round the self, of returning to the self or turning back on the self, the possibility of turning on oneself around oneself – the turn [*tour*] turns out to be it all [*tout*]. The turn makes up the whole and makes a whole with itself; it consists in totalizing, in totalizing itself, and thus in gathering itself by tending towards simultaneity; and it is thus that the turn, as a whole, is one with itself, together with itself. We are here at the same time around and at the center of the circle or the sphere where the values of ipseity are gathered together, the values of the together [*ensemble*], of the ensemble and the semblable, of simultaneity and gathering together, but also of the simulacrum, simulation, and assimilation. (Derrida, 2005b, 12; Derrida, 2003, 32)

Now, if the centre of the circle is abysmal, as both Beckett and Derrida saw it, it is because in its undecidable aporetic position of 'belonging' and 'not belonging' to the structure – while simultaneously being the most important part of it – it can take the place of both origin and end, *archè* and *telos*, as the infamous 'womb-tomb' in Beckett. At the same time, it is the structural point, as Derrida notices, from which 'repetitions, substitutions, transformations, and permutations are always *taken* in a history of meaning [*sens*] – that is, in a word, a history or story – whose origin may always be reawakened or whose end may always be anticipated in the form of presence' (Derrida, 1978, 352–3; 410).[17] As Amanda Dennis comments with regard to Molloy's counter-example: 'Rational subjectivity is figured as a dream with a thread, a story to tell' (Dennis, 2021, 91). In other words, the centre is the source, endpoint, and place of transmutation for all stories and plays because it is the point from which any story, either of meaning (like a philosophical or scientific discourse) or purely aesthetic (as work of fiction or even poetry) takes place. This is the reason why, in a contemplation of not only how such stories can be structured, but also of the fact that they cannot be structured without such a circular desire for the centre, namely in front of the painting in Erskine's room, Watt's stoic, almost machine-like demeanour finally breaks down, and his 'eyes filled with tears that he could not stem' (Beckett, 2006a, 273). While, in their turn, in front of such a centre, the hooded figures of *Quad I* and *II* continuously forget and anxiously evade it in their semi-perennial turns. If Chris Ackerley is right in seeing in the representation and distance of the broken circle and centre a figuration of different unbreachable gaps in Beckett ('the deep gulf separating Lazarus and Dives [. . .], or that between Murphy and the inmates of the MMM [. . .], the scholastic disjunction between *esse in*

---

[17] Italicised in the French original.

intellectu and *esse in re*, between man and God'; (Ackerley, 2006, 320), and if such a broken circle and looking/looked for centre is a synecdoche for most, if not all of Beckett's works, it is precisely because Beckett saw the aporias of phallogo-*centrism*, as Derrida exposed them since the late 1960s, in the conflation of reason and centre (as *Grund*). In other words, if, in the Attridge interview, Derrida was right in describing the particularity of Beckett's idiom in topological and figural terms beyond the themes, it is because he saw how the themes themselves of modernist literature were always determined by unknown or unthought structural and topological dimensions such as centre, circle, and turn, but also by their surfaces, ground (*Grund*), abyss (*Abgrund*), and so on. Hence, if the 'wombtomb' is a central figure in Beckett (like the skull and the desert), it is because it not only refers to the mother's body and the grave as analogical figures, but it also shows how our own figuration of such themes and the meanings we ascribe to them is not separated from the empirical and the imaginary spatialities and topologies we ascribe to them (inside, underneath, enclosed). What is more, there is no theme as a meaning of a story or discourse, without a pre-significant, synchronic pre-spatialisation in a proto-space or space before all spaces.[18] In other words, there is no theme or story without *khôra*.

2 *Khôra*: The Space of Genesis

Nowadays, in the era of the Anthropocene, the study of space in Beckett is understandably exploding. With two volumes in this Element series, Anna McMullan (2021) and Mark Byron (2020), and recent studies like Boulter (2020), Dennis (2021), James Little (2020), and Anthony Cordingley (2018), where space as a traditional philosophical category is prominent, Beckett's work appears to be a literary instantiation of how Derrida described *différance* in the homonymous conference of 1968, '*spacing*, the becoming-space of time, or the becoming-time of space' (Derrida, 1982, 13; 14), or as 'Text for Nothing VIII' describes it: 'time has turned into space and there will be no more time' (Beckett, 2006d, 320). However, as the different angles to the study of space in Beckett show, spaces here are not uniform, albeit they are all radical, or, at least, radically originary, showing 'the multiple surface manifest-ations of an abysmal deep structure whose laws, whose relation to meaning are unfathomable' (Moorjani, 1982, 64).

To return to our earlier analogy between Beckett's multiple beginnings in texts like *How It Is*, *Waiting for Godot*, *Not I*, *Play*, and so on, and those analysed by Derrida in Hegel's philosophical project, we can briefly examine a certain

---

[18] This is why, as Angela Moorjani expresses it, '*Watt*'s final fragment, "no symbols where none intended" [. . .] labels the novel as pre-symbolic play' (Moorjani, 1982, 39).

proto-space in the pre-beginning of Hegel's *Phenomenology of Spirit*, its preface or *Vorrede*, and compare it with some Beckettian genetic spaces. When, in this preface, Hegel is explaining the power of the *Understanding* as analysis, he describes it in contrast with an unbroken circle, and, after identifying such power with death, he spatialises the latter by making it into a passage or space through which Spirit must go in order to, accomplishing the turn, find itself. Here is the passage:

> The circle that remains self-enclosed and, like substance, holds its moments together, is an immediate relationship, one therefore which has nothing astonishing about it. But that an accident as such, detached from what circumscribes it, what is bound and is actual only in its context with others, should attain an existence of its own and a separate freedom – this is the tremendous power of the negative; it is the energy of thought, of the pure 'I'. Death, if that is what we want to call this non-actuality, is of all things the most dreadful, and to hold fast what is dead requires the greatest strength. Lacking strength, Beauty hates the Understanding for asking of her what it cannot do. But the life of Spirit is not the life that shrinks from death and keeps itself untouched by devastation [*Verwüstung*], but rather the life that endures it and maintains itself in it. It wins its truth only when, in utter dismemberment, it finds itself. (Hegel, 1977, 18–19)

This spatialisation of death is reinforced through the choice of the German term *Verwüstung* for devastation, a word that, like the Latin term *devastatio* – which entails the term *vastus* – includes the term for desert, *Wüste*.

As we can see, it is the contradictory trait of a broken-yet-reunited-circle before the beginning that links Hegel's devastation or desertification (*Verwüstung)* to Beckett's own inaugural post-apocalyptic deserts and desertic spaces. What is more, the discursive space itself of this devastation in Hegel, as prologue or before-discourse (*Vor-rede*), underscores space as a seminal and genetic dimension. In other words, such a devastation or radical emptying, being the original space of beginning, has no previous space to take place. Thus, as a space for space, it can only be what Plato called the third genre of beings (the first being the Idea and the second the sensible world), *khôra*: '*Khôra* everlasting, admitting no destruction, but affording place for all things that come into being' (Plato, 1903, 52a–b). As it appears in the *Timaeus*, *khôra* is a kind of cosmogonic surface or originary receptacle taking place – as a sort of place – at the utmost origin of the cosmos, between form and matter, or between what is modelled (matter) and the model (Idea). Like Schelling's *Grund* – which he developed, probably influenced by his early engagement with the *Timaeus* – hovering between an original ground or *Urgrund*, an effacing of the ground or *Ungrund*, and an abyss or *Abgrund*, *khôra* is the kind of surface or pre-surface before any inscription, which, aporetically, cannot be imagined without the future perfect ('it will have been marked') of its later inscriptions.[19] As the discursive structure of the *Timaeus* shows, given its aporetic status, it is very difficult to write *on* the subject of *khôra*, and whoever does it, as Plato does (through multiple voices in the dialogue), needs to – according to Derrida – *resemble* it in some way, if they want to raise this surface enough for us to perceive it:

> [Plato's] speech [*parole*] is neither his address nor what it addresses. It [*Elle*] *arrives* in a third genus and in the neutral space or a place without place, a place where everything is marked but which would be 'in itself' unmarked. Doesn't he already resemble what others, later, those very ones to whom one gives the word, will call *khôra*? (Derrida, 1995, 109; Derrida, 1993a, 59)[20]

In his own conception of an impossible original, originary, or first trace, Derrida links *khôra*, as this third genre of being as the originary or pre-originary place, surface, or receptacle, to Artaud's notion of the subjectile, an aesthetic pre-surface before any trait (plastic or discursive) can take place. Through this connection, he underlines not only the desire of the artist to remake or give birth to themselves, but also their divine or demiurgic trait as manipulators of *khôras* or proto-surfaces of inscription and impression. At the same time, he also emphasises Plato's own description of the supposition of *khôra* as a 'bastard reasoning' (νόθος) (52b), underscoring the necessary fictional character of such a presupposition (of the 'pre' of all positions), and giving us, in this way – through this recognition of the agnosic and structural necessity of *khôra* or the *subjectile* as proto-spaces – an inkling as to why Beckett's own idioms are inseparable from a proto-topology.[21]

As we know, *khôra* is not only translated as 'place' or 'receptacle', but also as 'mother' and 'wet nurse' or nourrice. As Paul Stewart and Mary Bryden, among others, have shown us, if Beckett's wandering characters are looking for and constantly finding something, these are receptacles (ditches, urns, jars, pots, and so on), and mother figures or wet nurses (Ruth-Rose, Lousse, Mag, Marguerite-Madeleine, Lulu/Anna, Molloy's mother, Mag, and so on). In other words, in Beckett's work there is a complicated, albeit essential, obsession with the

---

[19] Trezise underscores a similar belatedness of apparition in Derrida and Beckett but in terms of consciousness: 'consciousness belatedly manifests that which produces it and, as effect, becomes the cause of its own cause' (23).

[20] Derrida plays with the fact that the word '*parole*' (speech) is feminine to suggest an affinity between the feminine figure of *khôra* and Plato's speech.

[21] While Szafraniec sees the subjectile as a possible point of entry into a Derridean reading of Beckett, she misses the surface-like, *khôratic* dimension of the term, and thus its connection to the maternal body.

mother as the place or receptacle of pre-origin.[22] This is why, as we suggested earlier, *The Unnamable*'s most important and invariably first question is neither for the subject of the text, 'Who now?,' nor for its time, 'When now?' (both questions switching places between the two versions), but rather for its place: 'Where now?'[23] Or, as the unnamable underlines it, close to the end of the novel, after the voice promises 'No more stories from this day forth' (Beckett, 2006b, 378): 'seeking indefatigably, in the world of nature, the world of man, *where* is nature, *where* is man, *where* are you, what are you seeking, who is seeking, seeking who you are, supreme aberration, *where* you are' (379; my emphasis). In the original French version, this topological question becomes even more philosophical, even Kantian. Here, nature has lost its 'world', 'the world of man' is transformed into the faculty of 'the Understanding' (*l'entendement*), and the ancient Greek resounding term for 'being', '*on*' (ὄv), has brought up its universal place, effacing the particularity of 'you': 'cherchant toujours, dans la nature, dans l'entendement, sans savoir quoi, sans savoir *où*, *où* est la nature, *où* est l'entendement, qu'est-ce qu'on cherche, qui est-ce qui cherche, cherchant qui on est, dernier égarement, *où* on est' (Beckett, 1992, 164–5; my emphasis).

It is precisely this search for the originary place that, in the amalgamation of the mother and the pre-originary place of production or receptacle as *khôra*, makes the unnamable proffer, in 'the town of [its] youth' (Beckett, 2006b, 385), his matricidal desire: 'I'm looking for my mother to kill her, I should have thought of that a bit earlier, before being born' (385). At the same time, this amalgamation of the space of origin and the birthing or mothering body is what conditions all the aporetic configurations of the death/birth identification in the oeuvre, such as the 'not-having-been-born', the 'birth as death', 'astride of a grave', 'the wombtomb', and so on. As a remark again of the logic of the broken circle in search for its centre, this murdering/suicidal search for the originary place becomes the search for the ending place where I, as the narrative voice, am myself impossible – that is, the place of my own death. In other words, through the mother/son and the origin/end identification, the matricide is a suicide – and vice versa. As Derrida explains: 'Matricide forms a pair, so to speak, with infanticide. And since it is a child who tries to kill his mother, the matricide-infanticide leads on to suicide' (Derrida, 2013, 93).

Going back to the particularity of Beckett's idiom as a textual system that puts into play a *khôra* or *khôratic* spaces, we can ask: how exactly does this

---

[22] Brenda O'Connell underscores this essential Beckettian obsession with the mother too (2021, 108), albeit not through Derrida's but through Kristeva's *khôra*.

[23] Daniel Katz (1999, 29) and Van Hulle and Weller (2014, 173) have also remarked this topographic trait in *The Unnamable*.

resemblance between the text (and narrative voice) and *khôra* as original surface complicate any discourse on or story about it? In other words, how does such a structural and thematic amalgamation between text and genetic surface affect the determination of the text's or discourse's genre, since a discourse on *khôra*, or a chorology, is necessarily a genetic discourse on the origin of the origin itself and, consequently, on the original lack of distinction between genres, genders, characters, and determinations in this primordial ground? By giving figure to this primordial ground with the mud in *How It Is*, Beckett remarks not only the putatively first biological environment or life's genetic space, but also, in the indetermination of the words' origin (given that the novel presents itself as a long citation with an undetermined source), life's indistinction from discourse as Logos, the indistinction of nature from *technè*, as well as that between all speaking beings from each other.

Given this ur-indistinction or originary confusion, Beckettian stories or discourses on the original ground, like *How It Is*, are, as Mark Byron asserts of *Worstward Ho*, a 'literary cosmogony, a creation of a universe in language, but one subject to processes of geological erosion and agricultural accretion' (Byron, 2020, 54). The aporia of such a written cosmogony or chorology is that, by founding its own surface of inscription (or grounding its own ground like *Company* does, as Abbott suggests, as a 'Möbius strip'; 11), it does not give priority (grounding force) to any particular ground or original surface: neither to the earth as geological world or as ground of agri-culture, nor to the page as surface of inscription of its own – and any possible – discourse, nor to pure empty astronomical space as the original place of the cosmos. As the voice of *The Unnamable* expresses it – remarking again the necessary multiplicity at the origin, or what Derrida called its supplement – these, 'our beginnings collide [...] this place was made for me, and I for it, at the same instant' (Beckett, 2006b, 290). In other words, in their apparently simultaneous origins, neither of these grounds is *the* ground or place necessary for the others to take their place and begin.

An analogous kind of undecidability among original surfaces of inscription and textuality is present in Beckett's history of reading and note taking through the 1920s and 1930s. If, as Matthew Feldman notes, first 'Beckett was looking at developments and structures of thought within the Western philosophical tradition, especially its origins in Ancient Greece' (Feldman, 2006, 14), then turned to science and psychology, to psychoanalysis, and, finally to art theories like Franz Marc's and linguistic theories like Mauthner's, it is because these discourses also explore genetic surfaces. Philosophy focuses on the originary ground of thought and culture, psychology on the one of epistemology and the psyche, and art and linguistics examine the original grounds of personal and collective expression. If Beckett took notes on all these disciplines both consecutively and alternatively, it is because, in their explaining of the origins of things (both human and non-human), philosophy, psychology, science, linguistics, and art act consecutively and alternatively too as *Ur-*, *Un-*, and *Abgrund* of each other. That is to say, in their agonic efforts to explain humanity's origins and its original forces, especially with the development of different social sciences at the end of the nineteenth century – and with the waning of theology as a central study of civilisation – these discourses function as the original ground (*Urgrund*), the effacing of ground (*Ungrund*), and the abyss (*Abgrund*) of each other. In this way, they work as a system of inscriptions and effacements non dissimilar to those within and among texts like *Wortsward Ho*, *The Unnamable*, *Texts for Nothing*, *How It Is*, *Ill Seen Ill Said*, and so on, where scientific, mathematical, historical, and psychological discourses are sometimes parodied, sometimes mimicked, yet constantly questioned.

What the engagement with these different genetic discourses and disciplines means, in terms of the construction of the Beckettian oeuvre, is that, since Beckett built his works continuously with reference to the notes he took on these discourses and disciplines, his work is always reflecting on the aporias of these diverse origins and grounds of inscription. In other words, in most if not all of his work, Beckett continuously examines the developments and structures of thought, the world, and the self, not exactly at their beginnings, but rather as they are always constantly beginning and simultaneously failing to do so, like the self-deconstructing surfaces of the *Weltstoff* that interested him so much in the Presocratics, or like the third zone of Murphy's mind, where there are 'nothing but forms becoming and crumbling into the fragments of a new becoming, without love or hate or any intelligible principle of change' (Beckett, 2006a, 70). This is perhaps why, when considering the inextricable mesh of the origins of the psyche, the world, and thought on his notes on Windelband's explanation of Schopenhauer, he substituted the terms 'that dark, only on itself directed drive' ('*Jener dunkle,* [. . .] *Drang*') for the Schellingian 'the *Urgrund* und *Urzufall*' in the sentence: 'With him the <u>Urgrund</u> and <u>Urzufall</u> became the <u>will-to-live</u> and T I I [Thing-In-Itself]' (Beckett, 2020, 447; qtd in Feldman, 2006, 49–50). Through such a small substitution between the two philosophers' themes (Schopenhauer's dark drive '*dunkle … Drang*', and Schelling's original ground and accident '*Urgrund* and *Urzufall*'), he linked the Kantian Thing-In-Itself or noumena and the will-to-live with the originary ground and the originary accident that marks and turns the former into an inscribable surface. By doing this, the Beckettian idiom revealed that its secret or inaccessible core – its unnamable – was, as Derrida surmised, inseparable from its structure, its topology, and its inscribable *khôratic* or genetic surface.

Around 1938, a year before he died, Freud wrote: 'Spatiality might be the projection of the extension of the psychical apparatus. Probably no other derivation. Instead of Kant's a priori conditions our psychical apparatus. *Psyche is extended, knows nothing about it*' (Freud, 1946, 152; my translation and emphasis). Around the same time, in 1936, when considering angst and pain in relation to his own experiences, Beckett wrote (also in German):

> And that fear [of the incomprehensible] is truly completely incomprehensible, for its causes lie in the depths of the past, and not just in the past of the individual (in this case the task would perhaps not be insoluble and life would not necessarily be tragic), but of the family, the race, the nation, human beings, and nature itself. (qtd in Feldman, 2006, 112; UoR MS 5003/5)

'[I]n the depths', as any stratigraphic view can teach us, lie the original surfaces. If stratigraphy includes both lithostratigraphy and biostratigraphy, it is because at this place of absolute origin, the *Urgrund*, *khôra*, or the original extension as Beckett and Freud saw it, the psyche, the world, genders, genres, humans and nature cannot yet be separated, let alone individuated. In other words, 'in the depths of the past', the original surface or *khôra* is always the already marked Anthropocenic or post-apocalyptic one. Or as Hamm exclaims: 'The end is in the beginning (Beckett, 2006c, 141). Thus, as the unnamable realises it, this desire for the ultimate depths or *fonds* (a French term that can be translated as ground, bottom, background) has no end, since it is a perpetual form of haunting: 'Are there other pits [*fonds*], deeper down? To which one accedes by mine? Stupid obsession with depth [*profondeur*]' (Beckett, 2006b, 287; Beckett 1992, 10).[24]

Hence, if our era, the Anthropocene, defines the epoch where the surface of the Earth is indelibly written and constituted by human marks, and consequently, by the necessary effacing of the Earth as pre-original surface, the Anthropocene has always been there, here, since the beginning. Yet, if this always already-marked surface as Beckett raised it is the *khôra* or *Urgrund*, it means it is also, and simultaneously, the *Ungrund* and the *Abgrund*, the Un-grounding (or Un-reasoning) and the Abyss, the deathly centre of *Quad I* and *II*, but also of all structures, as Derrida explained them in his critique of structuralism. As such, what defines this original, abysmal ground (*Grund*) is not its grounding force, but the fact that all grounding and definition separating psyche and nature, epistemology and art, subjective and objective ground gets immediately effaced, blotted with each mark, in – as 'Text for Nothing VI' states it, paraphrasing the Gospel of John and Genesis – the 'slime where the Eternal breathed and his son wrote' (Beckett, 2006d, 314). As Derrida saw, it is precisely this aporia of the trace, where at the rising of the surface the inscriptions both reappear and disappear, that

---

[24] Beckett's unpublished fragment, '*Espace souterrain*' (1952), is another example of such obsession.

produces the desire for sense and story, namely, our own obsessions or the hauntologies that makes us who we are.

This is the desire of writing as both the drive to write at the beginning and what writing desires to achieve at and as the end. Beckett shows this arche-teleological aporia not only in the broken-circles of his texts and plays, in their semi-circular structures, but also in the insistent and repeated finality of his incipits, such as: 'I gave up before birth' (Beckett, 2006d, 411), 'For to end yet again [. . .]' (418), 'Birth was the death of him' (Beckett, 2006c, 453), 'till in the end / the day came' (462), 'Little is left to tell' (473), or in Malone's 'I am being given [. . .] birth to into death [Je nais dans la mort]' (Beckett, 2006b, 276; Beckett, 2004b, 177), and *Waiting for Godot*'s famous 'birth astride of a grave' (Beckett, 2006c, 82). This is also – as Derrida showed – the aporia of the fulfilment of the journey of Self-Consciousness as Spirit in Hegel's system, as the latter developed it in *The Phenomenology of Spirit* and the *Logic*.[25] For this process of Self-Consciousness to take place, Hegel must presuppose, *chronologically*, this desire for completion, this urge that compels it toward its end as *telos*. However, this means that such an end has to already be posited, *spatially*, at the other extreme of the book. At the same time, for Self-Consciousness and the reader to reach the end, *chronologically*, the desire that drives them there must already be inscribed, *spatially*, at the beginning of the book. It is this inversion in the spatialisation of time and the temporalisation of space – the play that Derrida called *différance* – that continuously reinscribes the end at the beginning, and vice versa. This is the rising of *khôra*, as the genetic surface on which any god or writer has written or marked anything, and whereupon they have also wished to finish (with) writing, and thus to erase what has been written. Given the meaning of *khôra* also as mother, this is the surface too of what Derrida called the logic of obsequence, according to which the mother will not only always precede the child, but also survive it. Finally, if, in Hegel, such an aporia between the beginning and the end describes the impossibility of the fulfilment of Self-Consciousness' knowledge, for Beckett, it describes the impossibility to end the, or even any story, and thus, the essential spectrality or hauntology of his work, at least – if Murphy is the last Beckettian character to effectively die in a narrative – from *Watt* on.[26]

---

[25] As Moorjani notices, there is a similar process of consciousness in Murphy's chess encounter with Mr. Endon, except that it is 'from consciousness, to self-consciousness to the unconscious' (Moorjani, 1982, 78).

[26] For an approximation of this unfulfilled 'bad infinity' of Hegel and Beckett, see Hans-Joachim Schulz (1973).

3 Hauntologies

Considering the development of Beckett's oeuvre, from his first narratives, to his last dramatic works on and for TV, the question of the rationale for his changes in media arises. If the move to the theatre can be explained by a visual and dramatic necessity, as well as an escape from the mental and linguistic isolation of fiction (as the writing of *Waiting for Godot* was from that of the trilogy), the move to television betrays another necessity. As Anna McMullan explains, 'the teleplays exploit the technologically mediated gaze of the television to intensify the uncanny effects of [the] ghosts of the Romantic tradition' (McMullan, 2021, 38). *What Where* provides an excellent example of this transformation, since the play's inherent structural and thematic spectrality benefited from the medium. Just as with the prose works and the dramatic pieces, where the medium of expression is at stake, structurally and thematically, Beckett's television plays question and utilise the televised medium in its singularity, exploiting especially what Derrida termed its 'hauntology'.

While a certain preoccupation with the ghost or spectrality began appearing in Derrida's works since *Truth in Painting* (1978), it is in *Specters of Marx* (1993) where he defines hauntology precisely in terms of telemedia and of a conjuration, as promise, between the public and the private. Such conjuration is:

> the act that consists in swearing, taking an oath, therefore promising, deciding, taking a *responsibility*, in short, committing oneself in a performative fashion – as well as in a more or less secret fashion, and thus more or less public, there where this frontier between the public and the private shifts constantly, remaining less assured than ever, as the limit that would permit one to identify the political. And if this important frontier is being displaced, it is because the medium in which it is instituted, namely, the medium of the media themselves (news, the press, tele-communications, techno-tele-discursivity, techno-tele-iconocity, that which in general assures and determines the *spacing* [*espacement*] of public space, the very possibility of the *res publica* and the phenomenality of the political), this element itself is neither living nor dead, present nor absent: it spectralizes. It does not belong to ontology, to the discourse on the Being of beings, or to the essence of life or death. It requires, then, what we call, to save time and space rather than just to make up a word, *hauntology*. We will take this category to be irreducible, and first of all to everything it makes possible: ontology, theology, positive or negative onto-theology. (Derrida, 2006b, 62–3; Derrida, 1993c, 89)

Given Derrida's cultural context as what the French call a '*soixante-huitard*' – an intellectual who developed his work through the crises and upheavals of French political and educational institutions that had their peak in 1968 – and his relative silence until the early 1990s on Marxism and Marxist theory,

Specters of Marx constituted not only an event in Derridean theory, but also somewhat of a response to an unspoken Marxist spectre in his oeuvre. Nevertheless, the notion of hauntology, together with the questions of the ghost and the spectre in the book, refer not only to the public/private televisual medium, to the spectres of Marxism at the end of the Cold War, when Fukuyama had declared 'the end of history', and to the infamous 'ghost of Communism' that circulates in Europe at the beginning of *The Communist Manifesto*, together with the spirits of Max Stirner, criticised by Marx and Engels in *The German Ideology*. Besides all these spectres, the main ghost in the book, framing it, is Hamlet's father's ghost.

As Beckett's scholars know, at least since Adorno's 'Trying to Understand Endgame', Beckett's work suffers from a deep Shakespearian hauntology in general, and, particularly, from *Hamlet*'s multifarious spectrality. As Claudia Olk has recently shown, Hamlet and its ghosts haunt Beckett's corpus since the beginning, particularly in the short story – unpublished during Beckett's lifetime – 'Echo's Bones', where the main character,

> Belacqua combines father, son and ghost, when he poses both as Hamlet, who suffers 'the slings and arrows of outrageous fortune' (*Ham* 3.1.58), and as old Hamlet's ghost, who is '[D]oomed for a certain term to walk the night' (*Ham* 1.5.10) until he has to yield to the 'sulph'rous and tormenting flames' (*Ham* 1.5.3) of Purgatory. (Olk, 2022, 79)

Furthermore, the spectrality and hauntologies particular to this, Shakespeare's most famous, if not his best play, extend all the way through Beckett's corpus, including in a work with a female protagonist, like *Happy Days*. As Olk explains:

> Beckett's scenery materializes her disembodiment and Winnie describes her disintegration as an echo of Hamlet's words: 'O that this too too solid flesh would melt, /Thaw and resolve itself into a dew' (*Ham* 1.2.129–30), to which she refers twice: 'and wait for the day to come [...] the happy day to come when flesh melts at so many degrees' (*CDW*, 144) as well as 'Shall I myself not melt perhaps in the end, or burn, oh I do not mean necessarily burst into flames [...] all this [...] visible flesh' (*CDW*, 154). Winnie not only metamorphoses into the material around her like Echo, but she also becomes the echo of Juliet and Imogen and voices Hamlet's longing for a transformative finality while being unable to act. (Olk, 2022, 91–2)

Now, if *Hamlet* frames *Specters of Marx*, it is not only because of Marx' predilection for Shakespeare – as underlined by Derrida – but also because the infamous ghost of Marxism and Communism, haunting Derrida himself, as a *soixante-huitard* at the end of the Cold War, is, like *Hamlet*'s and Beckett's own, a ghost of inheritance. In other words, as Beckett's early short story, 'Echo's

Bones', shows, with its subplot of Lord Gall's inability to have a male heir, and Belacqua's subsequent intervention, by becoming Lady Gall's lover himself, but 'wrongly' fathering a girl instead of a boy, spectrality or hauntology is always engaged with questions of inheritance. In other words, what haunts certain rulers, like Hamm or King Hamlet – as well as the sovereign leading Marxists and non-Marxist theorists and philosophers of the early 1990s – is who would inherit them or their kingdom. This haunting question of inheritance means that such a hauntology – like other dimensions shared by both Derrida and Beckett – is also connected with the questions of sexual difference and reproduction. This is clearly visible in 'Echo's Bones':

> The ghostly Belacqua becomes a son who is about to become a father in replacing the father who himself has become a ghost. He however breaks the unity suggested by the model of the Holy Trinity and ends the line of male heirs. (Olk, 2022, 80)

As we have seen, such a suspension of heritage happens not only through the lack of a son, but also and precisely through the birthing of a daughter *instead* of a male heir. Hence, if the question of sexual difference within the tradition of writing that includes both Derrida and Beckett – as both inheritors and ascendants – is another part of what made Derrida identify with Beckett, it is because both knew that the possibility of a different philosophical and literary inheritance involved a radical transformation of the tradition and its styles.

This question of the inheritance of deconstruction as a radical transformation of philosophical writing was indirectly asked to Derrida in the 2002 documentary *Derrida*, when, one of the directors, Kirby Dick, asked him, 'If you had a choice, what philosopher would you like to have been your mother?' (Dick and Kofman, 2005, 97). Here is his answer:

> DERRIDA (*smiling, bemused, addressing Amy*) That's his style, that's his own style? (*Pause*) I have no ready answer for this, give me some time. My mother? Good question, it's a good question in fact. I'll try to tell you why it's impossible for me to have any philosopher as a mother. My mother, my mother couldn't be a philosopher. [*Switching from English to French*]. A philosopher couldn't be my mother. That is very important. That says a lot of things. That means . . . that the figure of the philosopher is, for me . . ., and this is why also I am/follow [*je suis*] . . . I deconstruct philosophy; the figure of the philosopher is a masculine figure. And that is my problem. All the deconstruction of phallogocentrism is the deconstruction of what one calls philosophy which since its inception, has always been linked to a masculine and paternal figure. So, the philosopher is a Father, not a Mother. So, the philosopher that would be my mother would be a post-deconstructive philosopher, that is, myself or my son. My mother as a philosopher would have to be my granddaughter, for

example. An inheritor. A woman philosopher, who would have reaffirmed the deconstruction. And consequently, would be a woman who thinks, that's it, a woman who thinks. Not a philosopher ... but [who] thinks. I always distinguish thinking [*la pensée*] from philosophy, no? A thinking mother. That was crazy, that is what I try to ... it is the thing that I love, what I try to ... it's here ... from my birth, to try to give birth to ... to project. (Dick and Kofman, 2005, 97)

The end of this answer, with its reversibility, that is, having the male writer giving birth to his mother, describes well not only Beckett's own birthing of May Beckett through her incarnations in his oeuvre, but also the undecidable reversibility of birth (who gives birth to whom) within texts like *Footfalls*, or even *Ill Seen Ill Said*. What such reversibility exposes is not only the possible confusion expressed in V's question in *Footfalls*: 'Will you never have done ... revolving it all?' (Beckett, 2006c, 428) – a revolving similar to that of the turn described by Derrida in *Rogues*, trying to totalise and close the self while opening it to its other – but also the necessity to think of another kind of philosophical-literary inheritance, and consequently, of another tradition. For Derrida, this is the paradoxical maternal inheritance embodied in the logics of the obsequence and pregnancy. The first logic, as we saw earlier, prescribes that the mother will not only always precede the son/daughter, but that she will also always follow them, surviving them beyond their own death. The second one, playing with the notion of containment and receptacle, and thus, with *khôra*, implies that, given that one was contained in the womb, anything that one brings forth in life would already have been included in the mother.[27] Combined, these two logics speak of a survival and a comprehension of the maternal beyond all filial and paternal inheritances. In this way, these logics describe hauntology as a logic that – as Derrida explains – precedes any ontology, theology, and/or onto-theology, given that, being related to the mother, it bespeaks birth before being or even Being. In other words, such a hauntology is connected with *khôra* as the maternal pre-space of all origination or birth. Furthermore, if such a *khôratic*-hauntology takes the figure of the waking mother, as in Beckett's *Footfalls*, it is because even if in the matricidal dream of remaking oneself the author can kill the mother, according to Derrida, it would never be able to kill maternity itself. Because, following the logic of obsequence,

maternity always survives, as a revenant. She/It has the last word, and she/it wakes there. She/It wakes, this night watch, this vigil light, this nightlight

---

[27] This is why in the *différance*-slippage that Begam sees in Beckett, it is not only about one term (*nature/culture*, *narrator/narrated*) sliding into another, but about the container (*khôra*) inhabiting yet always overflowing the contained: 'inside becomes outside, agent becomes recipient' (Begam, 1996, 100).

[*veilleuse*], to use the word Trilling puts in capital letters ('*La Veilleuse*'!). It never sleeps; it not only keeps watch [*veille*] *over* the survivors but keeps vigil for them [*elle veille les survivants*]; it surveys them and survives them because those who come after it are also dead children, children who are already, like it/her, in the process of dying. Yes, matricide forms a pair with infanticide. (Derrida, 2013, 94; Derrida, 2001, 18–19).

If such a female and/or maternal hauntology and chorology appears better on a television screen, it is because, as Beckett shows, the space there is neither present nor absent, neither public nor private, neither masculine nor female.[28] Yet it is a place where visuality and sound, just like Narcissus and Echo, have their space of indecision. Such indecision remarks the essential trait that Derrida sees in the ghost and hauntology at large. This is an indecision embodied in the double referentiality of the genitive preposition '*de*' in the French syntax '*le fantôme* de *X*' ('the ghost *of* X'), according to which it is unclear who possesses or haunts whom: is the ghost of Hamlet its own image, its ghost appearing after Prince Hamlet is dead, or is it the ghost of somebody else's [his father] who haunts Hamlet because Hamlet has it? In Derrida's words:

> But does not a specter consist, to the extent that it consists, in forbidding or blurring this distinction? in consisting in this very undiscernability? Is not to possess a specter to be possessed by it, possessed period? To capture it, is that not to be captivated by it? (Derrida, 2006b, 132)

In Beckett's performative exploration of spectrality in his TV plays, such a suspension or indistinction takes, sometimes, an analogous form to the Narcissus/Echo myth. *Ghost Trio*, with its FEMALE VOICE and MALE FIGURE, is a perfect example. With its Echoesque, recorded female voice (distinguished, in its mechanicity or machine-like quality, by its refusal to change its tone or modulation), it begins the action by commanding the viewer to 'Look. [*Long pause*]. The familiar chamber' (Beckett, 2006c, 436), where the male figure will embody Narcissus in a double encounter with its own image. The first narcissistic reflection takes place in section II Action, from a broad point of view (A) that does not allow us to see his reflection, yet the voice partakes in the surprise:

21. *F turns to wall at head of pallet, goes to wall, looks at his face in mirror hanging on wall, invisible from A.*
22. *V: [Surprised.]* Ah!
23. *After 5 seconds F bows his head, stands before mirror with bowed head. 2 seconds.* (438)

---

[28] The question of the gender of the mother or the certain localisation of the maternal body in Derrida is complex; see 'The Night Watch' (Derrida, 2013).

The second narcissistic reflection takes place in the last section, III Re-Action, when the viewers get to partake too in the reflection, thus identifying them with him:

27. *Cut to close-up of F's face in mirror. 5 seconds. Eyes close. 5 seconds. Eyes open. 5 seconds. Head bows. Top of head in mirror. 5 seconds.* (441)

While this is the second reflection in the mirror, it is only the first one on the screen, since it is the first time that we, as viewers, get to see him, the male figure – and ourselves in him as a screen or mirror. What is more, near to the end, Beckett underscores this audience-character reflection by doubling it in a final one: '38. *Silence. F raises head. Face seen clearly for second time. 10 seconds*' (442). Thus the narcissistic reflection is complete, not only between the character and his image, but also between him, his image, and our own as viewers.

Such a performative reflection on narcissism is close to Derrida's own understanding of it, not as a self-centred tendency, but rather as a necessary reflection through another who, like Echo and the female voice in *Ghost Trio*, precedes Narcissus's own grief:[29]

> We are speaking about anything but narcissism as it is commonly understood: Echo, the possible Echo, she who speaks from, and steals, the words of the other, she who takes the other at his or her word, her very freedom preceding the very syllables of Narcissus, his mourning and his grief. (Derrida, 2005a, 24)

Moreover, as it happens in other works by Beckett (*Company, Waiting for Godot*, and so on), the narcissistic reflection is doubled again into a possible younger version of the male figure, a '*small boy*' (Beckett, 2006c, 441) who, after knocking, appears framed by the door, precisely between the first full narcissistic reflection in the mirror (between Male Figure – His Mirror Image – Us, the Spectators), and the last one (between the Male Figure and the viewer), when the face is '*seen clearly for the second time*' (442).[30] Besides constituting an anachronic reflection of self, this boy reinforces the stage of primary Narcissism as the *khôratic* or originary space whereupon identity will be built, and which, as a psychological neoteny, constitutes an infantile or youthful essence always threatening with partial or even total regression, and thus, with ultimate dissolution in a full return to the *khôratic* wombtomb.

The spectral suspension of the divide public/private is also exposed well in a play like *Eh Joe*, where the camera's approaching movement, together with

---

[29] As Daniel Katz describes it, the Beckettian 'narcissism' 'would consist of the appropriation of the echo of the other as oneself, as one's voice, which, in turn, could only make itself heard through its own disappropriation' (1999, 153).

[30] Anna McMullan also sees in this boy 'a younger version of [F's] self' (2021, 49).

the voice, act as an undecidable private/public accusation of guilt. The text voices some of the harshest accusations of an Oedipal drama, with Joe having 'throttled' his father, and to his mother, 'laid her too' (Beckett, 2006c, 393); the general accusation being, then, an utmost attempt to 'still' each one of an undefined 'us' – to which the voice belongs – until there's 'Not another one to still' (393). Furthermore, the final and hardest accusation of the play implies guilt on the suicide of a woman, described only as 'The green one .... The narrow one .... Always pale ....' (395). What is most striking about the form of Beckettian hauntology here is that, even if the guilt is suggested as a 'common' failed lover's guilt – the guilt of an impervious Don Juan – the most poignant charge lies on the utterance and effects of words and idiomatic expressions. Throughout the play, the voice quotes Joe with ironic compliments that nevertheless underline his guilt: 'The best's to come, you said' (392), 'Mental thuggee you called it' (393), 'That old paradise you were always harping on' (393), 'Voice like flint glass .... To borrow your expression' (394), and so on. At the end, however, the guilt of these more or less innocuous literary expressions becomes a murder accusation, as the voice connects one of Joe's idiomatic expressions, 'Spirit made light', with the aforementioned former lover's suicide: 'Spirit made light .... To borrow your expression .... The way [the eyes] opened after .... Unique' (395). The second time that the expression appears, the accusation reverts to the form of a question, as if to elicit a confession: 'Spirit made light .... Wasn't that your description, Joe?' (396). Finally, after the voice narrates the series of suicide attempts – until the successful one –, it turns into commands, and transforms Joe's expression into a pure idiom, a neologism: '*Imagine* the hands .... The *solitaire* .... Against a *stone* .... Imagine the *eyes* .... **Spiritlight** ....' (396; emphasis in original; my bold). Preceded by the direction '*Voice drops to whisper, almost inaudible except words in italics*' (396), the idiom almost exists like the 'a' of Derrida's 'La différance', 'a mute mark [...] a tacit monument, I would even say a pyramid' (Derrida, 1982, 4). It is 'purely graphic: it is read, or it is written, but it cannot be heard' (3). Or it can be heard barely – depending on the director and actor's choice – like a graphic, murderous idiom, surviving only on the script and the surface of Joe's face.

4 Living On

As Gontarski notes in his introduction to the Grove Press edition of *Nohow On*, there is a Derridean topological paradox in *Worstward Ho*: 'Can [the skull] then perceive itself if there is, to adapt Jacques Derrida, no outside the skull. From what perspective, from what grounding could it then be perceived?' (Gontarski,

1996, xxi). As the infamous quote from Derrida proclaims, 'there is nothing outside the text' (as Spivak translated it). In an analogous way, in *Worstward Ho* – if not in the whole *Nohow On* trifecta, and perhaps for all of Beckett's late works – there is no outside the skull. Less an immaterial Cartesian *res cogitans* and more a figuration of a Lacanian cross cap or torus, the skull in *Worstward Ho* is a singular – if somewhat folded or 'sunk' – surface of inscription and apparition without any outside, framed or tied, at its beginning and end, by its singular ritornello, 'on'.[31]

'On', this first and last word of *Worstward Ho*, underscores the aporia of its apparently infinite or boundless topology. There is no other place for this infinite place, this 'infinite here' (as 'Text for Nothing VI' describes it), or this 'Thenceless thitherless there' (Beckett, 2006d, 473) *on* which we appear, imagine, and write. In other words, there is no other surface (besides, perhaps, the surface of the reader's eye) from and on which we perceive, talk, or imagine the infinite surface of this 'on'.[32] This topological paradox foregrounds the *topos* or space as the essential dimension and question of these texts. As we have seen, this is what we can call Beckett's 'spacing of time' (as Derrida described *différance* in the homonymous conference), which, before the recent volumes on Beckett and space mentioned earlier (McMullan, Byron, Dennis, and so on), had been noticed already by Bruno Clément, for whom, Beckett 'turns the question of place into the question of writing' (Clément, 2009, 367), by Trezise in the context of Derrida's reading of Husserl (Trezise, 1990, 16–20), and by Gontarski, who sees in the *Nohow On* texts 'a reduction of narrative time to points of space' (Gontarski, 1996, xxvi).

On the other hand, when we describe what could be the key concept of Derridean deconstruction, we can agree with Martin Hägglund (2008) and decree *'espacement'* or 'spacing' as the main figure of Derrida's thought. What is more, given Derrida's insistence on the mark, trace, or even scratch (*graphos*) of any writing, sign, or impression – the condition of what he calls iterability –, such a 'spacing' cannot, like in Beckett's corpus, be conceived without a concrete, even if unstable, topology, as a logic of surfaces. In other words, there is no 'spacing', as well as no inscription, mark, or trace, without a surface or an 'on' as place of inscription, appearance, extension, movement, and, simultaneously, of effacement, disappearance, and stasis. In other words, there is no grammatology without a topography, and, most importantly, a chorology.

---

[31] Arka Chattopadhyay remarks this infinite and reflective topography of the skull in *Worstward Ho* (2018, 137).

[32] Accordingly, as Daniel Katz asserts, '"on", in some manner, transcends the category of possibility' (1999, 169).

Hence, Derrida's logic of grammatology and 'archi-writing' as generalised inscription describes the essential impossibility of being inscribed, of appearing, or of rising, *and* of – sometimes at the same time – being erased, disappearing, or of vanishing, without a surface. Such a logic of topological and topographic necessity is performatively examined, and tried, in *Worstward Ho*. Given this necessity of the surface, as the text explores it, there is an aporia between an inerasable immortality or an impossibility to simply disappear ('Nothing ever unseen'; 'Never to naught be brought. Never by naught be nulled'; Beckett, 2006d, 477, 479), and an inevitable, constant effacing or sinking in on the void ('Alone in the dim void'; 477). This logic of the persistence of the surface[33] as the structure *on* which everything takes place – or where everything stops having its place – was described further by Derrida in 'Living On: *Border Lines* ', a text examining Blanchot's *La folie du jour* and *L'arrêt de mort*, a novella comprising two stories that narrate the death of two female characters, J. and Nathalie, the first one of whom goes through a resurrection. Reflecting, in this text – titled in French, *Survivre* – on the enduring that Blanchot sees in surviving, Derrida glosses on the 'on' (*sur*) of 'living on' (*survivre*), and on how it continuously recreates a topos in between living and dying, that is to say, a spatio-temporal suspension or *epochè*, analogous to the genetic and spectral topology we find in *Worstward Ho*:

> This enduring, lasting, going on, stresses or insists *on* the 'on' of a living on that bears the entire enigma of this supplementary logic. Survival and *reve-nance*, living on and returning from the dead: living on goes beyond both living and dying, supplementing each with a sudden urge and a certain reprieve, deciding [*arrêtant*] life *and* death, ending them in a decisive *arrêt*, the *arrêt* that puts an end to something, and the *arrêt* that condemns with a sentence [*sentence*], a statement, a spoken word, or a word that goes on speaking. (Derrida, 2004, 89)

These sentences as *arrêts*, simultaneous life and death sentences, appear in *Worstward Ho* – and in *Company* and other texts, like *Imagination Dead Imagine* – in the form of commands for the Reason, the Imagination, and the depths of this faculty, where Kant's schemata are formed. These are impossible – or what Derrida calls 'double bind' – commands prescribing the simultaneous appearance and disappearance of figures and their space. The 'on' – common English transla-tion of the French preposition '*sur* ', as well as phonetic transcription of the ancient Greek word for 'being' (ὤν) – gives figures to both, the sentence as command or imperative, and to a multifarious topology that includes the space of sight (stare), the surface of the word (say), and the *khôratic* pre-surface of being (be) and its

---

[33] Shane Weller (2005) does a similar reading of persistence or 'survival' by approaching *Worstward Ho*'s 'unlessenable least' and Derrida's 'remains'.

modalities: 'On. Stare on. Say on. Be on. Somehow on. Anyhow on' (Beckett, 2006d, 477). In this way, the survival as 'living on' in the text appears as a simultaneous genesis of a space and a sentence, in an analogy and reinterpretation of the cosmogonies described in both Genesis ('And God *said*, Let there be light: And there was light'; Gen. 1:3; my emphasis) and John ('In the beginning was the Word, and the Word was with God, and the Word was God'; John 1:1). For his part, Derrida sees a similar simultaneity of word and act in Blanchot's *L'arrêt de mort*, where 'Thus the *récit* will be the cause – as well as *causa, chose* [thing, mere tool] – of what it seems to recount. The récit as the cause and not as the relating of the event: this is the strange truth that is announced. The récit's the thing' (Derrida, 2004, 118).

This causality or simultaneity between the words and the acts is suggested to Derrida, in 'Living On', by the aforementioned resurrection of the character of J., who, even though she will ultimately die at the end of the first of two stories, comes back to life at the exact moment the narrator calls her, without a pause between the two events ('there wasn't a second's interval' (Blanchot, 1978, 20). In a similar confusion of the origin of voices as in *Company* or *How It is* – and through a simultaneity that reminds us too of the echoed lines in *Rockaby*, spoken by both, the recorded voice and the woman in the chair ('time she stopped', 'living soul', 'rock her off') –, here one does not know, ultimately, who calls whom:

> Resurrection, birth, or triumph of life thus will not have been the effect of a cause, but rather an absolute event, a cause even, the cause, the *causa, la Chose*, the first name itself: since now no interval or interruption separates the call from the first breath, we do not even know anymore who pronounced the name for whom. (Derrida, 2004, 103)

As a genetic, 'conceptual', or 'birthing' text, namely, as a text constituted and remarked as a pure act of creation or conception – or, as Amanda Dennis describes it, 'a parable of the authorial process in the absence of an external creator' (Dennis, 2021, 197) – *Worstward Ho* appears too as an absolute event instead of a representation. It is thus a thing (*chose*), or just a 'name' (the Beckettian idiom in the title, 'worstward ho!', underscoring this singularity), especially remarked by its untranslatability, even to its own bilingual author. It appears thus as one of Beckett's final idioms, a finality stemming not only from the closeness in time to its author's death, but also because of the closed perfection of its idiom, in other words, because of its impossibility – and desire – to be translated or said otherwise.[34]

---

[34] Beckett expressed such a perfection as fulfilment and ending in a letter to André Bernold (the person responsible for the inclusion of Derrida's *Ulysse gramophone* in Beckett's library) from 19 May 1983: 'I think that *Worstward Ho* has finished me off (*m'a achevé*)' (Beckett, 2016, 610–11).

Nevertheless, as the (unwarranted by the tenor of the whole of Beckett's oeuvre)[35] fame of the two short quotes, 'Try Again. Fail Again. Fail Better' (Beckett, 2006d, 471) and 'you must go on, I can't go on. I'll go on' (Beckett, 2006b, 407) shows, there is, in *Worstward Ho* – as in *The Unnamable*, and other texts – a persistence, an insistence, or continuation, not disconnected from a logic of survival. Going back to J.'s resurrection, Derrida connects it too – indistinguishable from the narrator's call – with the end of the second story, and thus of the whole book or novella, where the narrator, taking advantage of the feminine gender of the word 'thought' in French (*la pensée*), talks about a certain thought, stronger than himself, in terms that make it seem that he is talking about a certain 'her', whom, at the exact end, he calls 'eternally' – as he has done before (or they, since it is impossible to decide if the two male narrators of the two stories are the same one) – and to which she responds 'eternally' as well:

> As for me, I have not been the unfortunate messenger of a thought (*pensée*) stronger than I, nor its toy, nor its victim, because that *thought*, if it (*elle*) has conquered me, has only conquered through me, and in the end has always been at my same measure. I have loved it/her and I have loved only it/her, and everything that happened I wanted to happen, and having had regard only for it/her, wherever it/she was or wherever I might have been, in absence, in unhappiness, in the inevitability of dead things, in the necessity of living things, in the fatigue of work, in the faces born of my curiosity, in my false words, in my deceitful vows, in silence and in the night, I gave it/her all my strength and it/she gave me all its/her strength, so that this strength is too great, it is incapable of being ruined by anything, and condemns us, perhaps, to immeasurable unhappiness, but if that is so, I take this unhappiness on myself and I am immeasurable glad of it and to that thought, to her/it, I say eternally, 'Come', and eternally it/she is there. (Blanchot, 1978, 80; qtd in Derrida, 1986, 218).

This confusion, in Blanchot's story, between an indeterminate her and *a* thought – or 'thought' in general –, that makes the author think, imagine, and write, also gives figure to the insistence of female voices and presences haunting male characters in Beckett's late texts like *Eh Joe, Ghost Trio, Ill Seen Ill Said, Nacht und Träume*, and *. . . but the clouds . . .,* as well as to the feminine voices themselves trapped in loops or semi-loops of speech, like Mouth in *Not I*, May in *Footfalls*, and Winnie in *Happy Days*. However, it is in *Worstward Ho*, where the undisentangeable confusion between speech, word, writing, creation, imagination, and conception, and their simultaneous coming to be, takes place. In this way, the text, whose title – connected to the 1855 maritime novel *Westward Ho!* – wakes up images of an ocean, appears as a living cosmogonic surface, or a new avatar of the primeval or infernal mud of *How It Is*. In other

---

[35] For a reconsideration of the potential optimism of Beckett's lines, see Eva Kenny (2020).

words, as a genetic or cosmogenetic text, *Worstward Ho* works as a *khôra*. Or, given this Greek term's connection with the mother-receptacle as both the simultaneously genetic surface sustaining and letting the world rise, *and* as the depths, or the ultimate lack of surface – the abyss engulfing it all – *Worstward Ho* appears also as 'the deep', upon whose waters or face God's spirit moved at the beginning of Genesis.[36] In the original Hebrew, this deep or abyss is called *tehom* (ההום), a word potentially related to the name of the Mesopotamian goddess, Tiamat, another victim of a kind of matricide (by her great grandson Anu), and whose body becomes the material (*mater*) for the creation of the cosmos (form). Thus, beyond the reminiscences of an oceanic surface it recalls (related to Beckett's recurrent images of the water at the seawater baths in Dún Laoghaire, of the lake on which Krapp and his companion drifted, and of Molloy's beach), the writerly surface or topography of *Worstward Ho* is also the deeps of the faculty of the Imagination for Kant, where the schemata are born, and out of which – and on which, as page or canvas – they are drawn. In other words, *Worstward Ho*'s depth, from which everything oozes, is where the unions between intuitions, perceptions, images, words, and concepts are conceived. Thus, on this cosmogonic surface, before any such union – allowing speech, writing, and images to be formed – arises, the only thing that is possible is itself as surface: *on*.

However, because Beckett was not exactly Kant, the figures that come out of this cosmo- and epistemogonic space or *khôratic* surface as 'schemata', are not regular categories, but One – 'the kneeling one', Two – 'the twain', and Three – 'the head' (Beckett, 2006d, 475). Given that, at least, the first two are gendered ('an old woman's', 'an old man and child'; 480, 473), this space of conception includes and takes account of sexual difference. However, like in the earlier story 'Enough', where the sex/gender of a character is not suggested until the end, the revelation of One, 'the kneeling one' or 'bowed back' (476) as an old woman does not happen until after the first half of the text. What is more, as the first figure to appear in the text – simultaneously or, in other words, genetically indistinguishable with its place ('First the body. No. First the place. No. First both'; 471) – it is, precisely, as bones that are ground that it surges, reminding the Beckettian reader of Echo, Narcissus' sempiternal pendant: 'Say bones. No bones but say bones. Say ground. No ground but say ground' (471). On the other hand, when considering the goal or desired process of worsening the text – namely, of their preying one on the other ('All always faintly preying'; 483) – of the

---

[36] For this reversibility between surface and abyss in the *khôratic* surface, see my 'Between the Ocean and the Ground: Giving Surfaces' (Martell, 2024a).

three numbers it is Two, 'the twain', 'the old man and child', representing not only filiation and masculine inheritance or genealogy, but also the survival or living on of the infant dimension, that proves the most recalcitrant: 'What of all seen and said not on them preying? True. True! And yet say worst perhaps worst of all the old man and child' (479). However, at the end, this pseudo-Oedipal trinity (old woman, old man, and child) gets reduced to a singular, purportedly sexless one, through the genderless skull: 'Two black holes in foreskull. Or one. Try better still worse one. One dim black hole mid-foreskull. Into the hell of all. Out from the hell of all' (483–4).

Beckett's logic of survival or 'living on' in *Worstward Ho* is thus a complete re-creation of language through new idioms ('worstward ho', 'unstillable', 'unlessenable', and so on, but also all the idiomatic syntax of the text), or a full reappropriation and recreation of English as of his mother tongue (alienated through the passage to French), in order to try and make it untranslatable and yet translatable. As Derrida remarks, such living on or *sur-vivre* of the text happens only in the simultaneity of the aporia of its translatability and its untranslatability: 'A text lives only if it lives *on* {*sur-vit*}, and it lives *on* only if it is *at once* translatable *and* untranslatable (always "at once . . . and . . . ": *hama*, at the "same" time)' (Derrida, 2004, 102). As with other Beckett's texts – like the published separately fragment from *How It Is*, 'The Image' – such desired simultaneity appears in a synchronicity more appropriate to painting and the visual arts than to writing and the diachronic: 'All at once in that stare' (Beckett, 2006d, 476), 'All at once as one' (484). Nevertheless, for this synchronicity to take place, it needs, like the eternally answering she (*elle*) or thought of Blanchot's *L'arrêt de mort*, a certain, if not eternity, at least 'oncelessness'. In *Worstward Ho*, there is only one such element: 'Onceless alone the void' (481). In the constant creation and erasure of all the elements, in their changes and lack of change: 'Void cannot go' (475). This is why at the end of the text, when the three figures and everything else get reduced to the one hole, there is no going beyond the limits of the limitless void: 'Three pins. One pinhole. In dimmest dim. Vasts apart. At bounds of boundless void. Whence no farther' (485). Yet, if the void has an essential characteristic, it is that, like *khôra*, it allows for something to stand: 'It stands. See in the dim void how at last it stands' (472).

In the void of its untranslatability, standing, constantly demanding to be translated, Beckett's texts continue 'living-on', as Derrida remarked with Walter Benjamin, through a translation of '*übersetzung*' that always potentially implies both: '*überleben*' (living over or past the death of the author, his parents, children, and so on) and '*fortleben, living on*, continuing to live' (Derrida, 2007, 26).

5 Deconstructing the Sovereign Subject

'Tears and Trembling'

Beckett's first published short story, 'Assumption', tells the story of a male character's sonic explosion. While at the beginning, the eruption is described as an aporetic possibility ('He could have shouted and could not'; Beckett, 2006d, 57), at the end, after he meets the woman who, silently, will come into his life to help him release the explosion, it is an impersonal event, described in the one before the last paragraph with the neutral: 'Then *it* happened' (60; my emphasis). Such a sonic event, as Beckett describes it, shakes 'the very house' where it takes place 'with its prolonged, triumphant vehemence' (60). However, before this architectural shaking due to the force of an orgasmic scream takes place, and even before the apparition of her, the woman who will 'loosen yet another stone in the clumsy dam set up and sustained by him' (60), the main character wonders if the rebellious pent-up scream within himself had ever provoked a bigger trembling, that of God or 'the Power' itself:

> In the silence of his room he was afraid, afraid of that wild rebellious surge that aspired violently towards realization in sound. He felt its implacable caged resentment, its longing to be released in one splendid drunken scream and fused with the cosmic discord. Its struggle for divinity was as real as his own, and as futile. He wondered *if the Power* which, having denied him the conscious completion of the meanest mongrel, bade him forget his fine imperfection beside it in the gutter, *ever trembled at the force of his revolt.* (58; my emphasis)

Thus the force and trembling are adjudicated undecidedly to both the male character and it, the scream. 'Its struggle' is 'his revolt', and both aspire futilely for divinity and/or completion. What is more, they aspire not only to release their tremors but also to make the Creator or creating Force tremble as well. As one would expect – especially given the remains of unanimist tendencies in Beckett –, if, at the end, there is a fusion between the sonic explosion ('great storm of sound'; 60) and the forest and the sea, such fusion can only spell the death of the character. Thus, even though, through his sexual encounters with the woman he did experience, every night, a type of apotheosis ('each night he died and was God'; 60), at the end, there was no other divine trembling besides his own.

For such an early text, it is impressive how Beckett had already identified one of his main and lasting conundrums: the question of an embodied yet impersonal force or necessity making him – and his characters – speak, yell, sing, or write a 'final word' or 'quoi'. This is the question and structure of one of Beckett's last texts, the poem 'Comment dire'/'What is the word', where in a classic Beckettian mixing of epistemological and ontological questions, what needs to be said, or the word one is looking for, lingers between a general or private given of the world ('given all this'; Beckett, 2000, 274), a phenomenon or the base of phenomenology as appearing ('seeing all this this here' 274), and a modal experience arising from a particular place ('folly for to need to seem to glimpse afaint afar away over there what' 276). Such a search for the undecidably private or public word or words reveals itself as a search for a secret that – like the 'dear name' in *Ohio Impromptu*, the searches between different circles and centres in *Watt*'s painting, the 'fin mot enfin'/'the key' (Beckett, 1984b, 43; Beckett, 2006d, 461) in *Ill Seen Ill Said*, or the abyss or *Abgrund* in *Quad I* and *II* – lies undecidable between the private or silent, and the public or sayable, or between being a secret as an object one *has* and as the secret core of what the subject *is*; like Krapp's and Beckett's shared dark, or what both 'always struggled to keep under' (Beckett, 2006c, 226). For Derrida, such a secret is an essential part of deconstruction. It marks the secret place of a lack of transcendence that – like the coffer and trapdoor in *Ill Seen Ill Said* – by keeping, even if empty, the space or location for such a transcendence, negates pure unaffected immanence or a purely empirical world. Derrida described it, in a late interview with *Les Temps modernes*, in terms reminiscent of the empty centres of Beckett's texts which, be them literal, like the centre of *Quad I* and *II*, or nominal, like Godot himself, are the thing, *la chose*, or what makes the characters and writer speak, inscribe, write, and, ultimately, go on. For Derrida:

> in the work of deconstruction, something similar exists: a movement to enunciate, say, or write something related to a secret, but to which we do not have access, to which we will never have access. Perhaps there isn't even a secret – that's the secret – perhaps there's *nothing*: no God, no religion, no unconscious, *nothing*. But *this nothing* is still something. It's still **a void around which I turn**, a secret void that makes me speak without knowing what it's about: X. (Derrida and Ben-Naftali, 2017, 171; 50; emphasis in original; my bold)

Such a questioning of the place of God, religion, the unconscious, and so on, appears as well in both oeuvres, and not only through the obvious resonances with religious imagery and questions: God-ot, Beckett's constant biblical references, both textual and visual, Derrida's and Beckett's discursive and performative interest in negative theology and apophatic discourse, their own engagements with the ontotheology of our Greco-Roman-Judeo-Christian-Muslim cultures, and so on. It also appears through the structural and thematic utilisation of a potentially transcendent, secret dimension or element that, nevertheless, is always suspended. In other words, in their ontologies and epistemologies, there is a transcendent – albeit not necessarily religious – element that is never neither completely affirmed nor denied.

As a functional element, such oozing of transcendence affects their discourses, making them continuously pause and correct themselves, following
the logic of epanorthosis that Bruno Clément examines in *L'Œuvre sans
qualités*. It makes them, as Derrida said of Freud in *Beyond the Pleasure
Principle*, speculate and state continuously – as in *How It Is* – 'something
wrong there'. In other words, it makes them limp, shiver, tremble, and stutter.
As it happens with the violent shaking in 'Assumption', and the broken syntax
of 'Comment dire'/'What is the Word', or in the myriad of skewed speech and
thought patterns in Beckett's work, this transcendent place or figure, as the place
of a secret without a determinable source, not only makes the narrators speak or
write, but it also makes them tremble and shake while doing it, transforming any
assured speech – like Lucky's academic discourse – into a pathological, frag-
mented, hiccupped soliloquy. Because, when one trembles while talking, as
Derrida explains: 'It is as if "I" started babbling, stammering, not being able to
find or form its words, as if "I" stuttered, incapable to finish the self-positional
phrase that is interrupted precisely by the trembling' (Derrida, 2006a, 95; my
translation). Given this trembling *Logos* (speech, writing, and thought), such
a difficulty to state an auto-positional phrase reaffirming the speaker/writer
affects not only the syntax and the topic of the characters' discourses, but also
their identities, making them question them and, ultimately, lose any stable
position and, sometimes, metamorphose continuously.[37] As we know, such
metamorphoses happen both within singular texts (*Malone Dies*, *The
Unnamable*), and in a series of works (*Murphy*, *Watt*, *Molloy*, *Malone Dies*,
The Unnamable, *Texts for Nothing*, and so on), becoming an essential part of the
whole oeuvre.

It is this shaking impossibility to calmly auto-position one-self that, ultimately, grounds Beckett's ethical stance of non-compromise, linking it to
Derrida's ethics of self-deconstruction. As Jean-Michel Rabaté explains:
'Beckett's strenuous efforts as a writer help us reject pseudo-values and reach
a site – a linguistic and ethical *position* – in which one can truly think, love, live,
or write' (Rabaté, 2016, 3–4; my italics). Ultimately, this means that the position
for such truths or true experiences is necessarily unstable. Its stance must be
a shaking, a stuttering. In other words, the Beckettian ethical and aesthetic site is
a site of quakes, both of the *khôratic* Earth and of the self. For both Derrida and
Beckett, such a tremor or trembling must be fundamental, in the sense that it
shakes not only all the assurances of the self, but also of the ultimate foundations, reasons, or grounds, the *Grund* of German Idealism, and the fond

---

[37] Such a trembling is also part of the reification of different-abled bodies present in Beckett's
work; see Hannah Simpson (2022a and 2022b).

(background, depth) of philosophies like Deleuze's (see Deleuze, 1976). For Derrida, without such an ultimate shaking or tremor there is no thinking, as well as no responsibility, since such trembling is the manifestation of the lack of pre-programmed structure, in other words, of an already made or programmed decision or thought, which hinder any real decision or thought. Just as a decision should not be programmed in order to be a decision, nor a thought preconceived, such trembling must happen, as with many events in Beckett's work, suddenly. Consequently, it must spell not only personal tremors, but also the shaking of the whole Earth. It is thus never just an 'I shake' or 'I self-deconstruct', but an 'it shakes', 'it deconstructs itself'. In other words, as one of Derrida's favourite Celan's verses expresses it, such a terrestrial shaking pronounces: '*die Welt ist fort*' (the world is gone/far), which is the opening or necessary condition of possibility for the next line of the poem, spelling the absolute responsibility toward the other: '*ich muss dich tragen*' (I must carry you). In Derrida's own words:

> I am not only thinking about the trembling of the ego, but also about the trembling of the ground, of the entire ground, the foundation, about the trembling of the earth as the collapsing of the ground, of the foundation, of the *Grund*, a trembling happening all of a sudden, and there [*là*] where one no longer knows what to rest upon. And this is the typical, archetypal, even archaeological situation of deconstruction. Deconstruction is when something *deconstructs itself* [*ça se déconstruit*]. All of a sudden, there is no longer any foundation, there are no longer any guaranteed axioms, there is no longer any assured terrain, *die Welt ist fort*, the world itself, the world as earth, as foundational ground, is no longer assured. I think that one only ever starts thinking within this trembling. All of a sudden, nothing is assured anymore, nothing is solid anymore. But I'll also say that this experience is always an experience of responsibility. [...] If I took responsibility while being tranquil and did only what needed to be done, knowing that that's my duty – thus, if I took responsibility without trembling – well, this would not be, or would no longer be, responsibility. I would be applying a program, a technique. So, there is never any true responsibility without trembling. One trembles when one makes a decision, whatever decision it may be. Sometimes it's an insignificant decision, but sometimes they are tragic decisions. And one must tremble. All of a sudden, body and ground tremble. (Derrida and Ben-Naftali, 2017, 169–70; Derrida, 2012, 48–9)

Perhaps there is no better exemplification of such a trembling as an opening for both ethics and aesthetics in Beckett's work, than *Ill Seen Ill Said*. In the barren landscape of this text, affected by a quiet but continuous earthquake, the Derridean structure of care when the world is gone, expressed by Celan's lines '*die Welt ist fort, ich muss dich tragen*', takes place, with the twelve guardians – and the eye – watching over the old woman. What is more, such a generalised trembling relates to a performative reflection on tears as a different use of the eyes and of vision at large. The dazed eye, cause of the 'ill seen', is thus seen not as a limitation of a rightful use, to see (the essential sense in scientific investigation), but rather as an instantiation of Derrida's hypothesis, according to which:

> deep down inside, the eye would be destined not to see but to weep. For at the very moment they veil sight, tears would unveil what is proper to the eye. And what they cause to surge up out of forgetfulness, there where the gaze or look looks after it, keeps it in reserve, would be nothing less than *aletheia*, the *truth* of the eyes, whose ultimate destination they would thereby reveal: to have imploration rather than vision in sight, to address prayer, love, joy, or sadness rather than a look or gaze. Even before it illuminates, revelation is the moment of the 'tears of joy'. (Derrida, 1993b, 126)

This is why for Beckett's narrators there is a confusion in their *Logos* between their discourse and their tears: 'It's an unbroken flow of words and tears [. . .] I confuse them, words and tears, my words are my tears, my eyes my mouth' (Beckett, 2006d, 320). In the world of *Ill Seen Ill Said*, such a crying is essentially connected to – if not another manifestation of – the generalised, even if imperceptible, earthquake, and to the figure of Christ and his sacrifice through the ichthys, the pisciform buttonhook hanging on the wall, indirect sign and measure of the Earth's tremblings:

> Weeping over as weeping will see now the buttonhook larger than life. Of tarnished silver pisciform it hangs by its hook from a nail. It trembles faintly without cease. As if here without cease the earth faintly quaked. [*A peine*: barely] [. . .] Since when it hangs useless from the nail. Trembling imperceptibly without cease. (Beckett, 2006d, 455; 21–2)[38]

If, as Derrida described it, in this world, the eye's truth and destination is imploration and prayer – 'if she prays' (Beckett, 2006d, 463) – it is not the religious prayer to a certain god, but rather, as Beckett expressed it in a letter to McGreevy, it is the prayer as poem, because, '*in the depths where demand and supply coincide* [. . .] the prayer is the god. Yes, prayer rather than poem, in order to be quite clear, because *poems are prayers*, of Dives and Lazarus one flesh' (Beckett 2009, 274; my emphasis). If the space of this equivalence is 'the depths', it is because there, where the tectonic plates crash, lies the origin of all the quaking and tremors – and, simultaneously, of all stupidity or haunting: 'Stupid obsession with depth' (Beckett, 2006b, 287; 10).

At the end of *Samuel Beckett: Laughing Matters, Comic Timing*, when considering the overall shape of Beckett's work as that of '"perhaps", of "strong

---

[38] Words in square brackets appear only in the French version.

weakness", of tremor', Laura Salisbury quotes one of – the already referenced –
Derrida's direct statements on Beckett, when the philosopher describes the
writer as an artist who – among others – makes 'the limits of our language
tremble' (qtd in Kearney, 1995, 162). This figure of trembling or tremor was
recurrent in Derrida's writing since the beginning, when he examined, for
example, how Hegel saw in trembling (*Erzittern*) 'the first and most ideal breath
of the soul [*Seelenhaftigkeit*]' (Derrida, 1982, 92, 107). The tremor gained in
prominence, however, at the end of Derrida's career, with his last public
intervention being titled 'How to avoid trembling?'. As Salisbury explains,
such a tremor is part of a descriptive not prescriptive ethos in Beckett, a 'strong
weakness' that questions knowledge. This is the reason why Beckett embraced
Guelincx's *nescio* (I don't know), instead of Descartes' *cogito* (I think), both in
the form of what I can (ill) see, and of what I can (ill) say. It is also why a non-
epistemological epoch appears as the utmost dream in works like *Ill Seen Ill
Said*, an epoch that cancels the questions and the thirst for knowledge, while,
sporadically, annulling also the impossibility not to want to know:

> Was it ever over and done with questions? [*Fut-il jamais un temps où plus
> question de questions?*] Dead the whole brood on sooner hatched. Long before.
> In the egg. Long before. Over and done with answering. With not being able.
> With not being able not to want to know. With not being able. No. Never.
> A dream. Question answered. (Beckett, 2006d, 462; Beckett 1984b, 46).

This is a dreamt epoch that has resigned to, as Derrida wrote: 'wanting to have
the power to see and to know [*vouloir avoir le pouvoir de voir et de savoir*] – and
you can manipulate this chain in <all> directions' (Derrida, 2009, 281; Derrida,
2008, 377).

If, in Beckett's worlds such as *Ill Seen Ill Said*'s, the Understanding and
Reason as the faculties of knowledge are shaken in their foundations, it is thus
the Imagination, or as the misattributed sentence – by Voltaire – to Malebranche
called it, 'la folle du logis' (the madwoman of the house) who reigns alone in
a teary realm.[39] This faculty as a 'madwoman in the house' is directly analo-
gised with the female protagonist of *Ill Seen Ill Said* through Beckett's translation of the original French line 'La folle du logis s'en donne à coeur chagrin'
(Beckett, 1984b, 21) to 'Imagination at wit's end spreads its sad wings'
(Beckett, 2006d, 455). Thus, the 'Imagination' of texts produced in the 1960s
like 'All Strange Away' and 'Imagination Dead Imagine' gets here embodied in
a weeping female figure, coming from the Enlightenment through Voltaire – or,
following the text, from an immemorial past, like *khôra* – and revealing the

---

[39] Nevertheless, in a text like *Company* Beckett underscores how the faculty of Imagination is
never detached from the other Kantian faculties.

eye's true emotive and not epistemological function. If the text is conscious of the voracious and potentially murderous drive of its gaze ('Quick again to the brim the old nausea and shut again. On her. Till she be whole. Or abort'; Beckett, 2006d, 462; Beckett, 1984b, 47), it also questions the possibility of another kind of perception, apprehension, and self-apprehension, and consequently, of another kind of necessity and of the utterable:

> What is it defends her? Even from her own. Averts the intent gaze. Incriminates the dearly won. Forbids divining her. What but life ending. Hers. The other's. But so otherwise. She needs nothing. Nothing utterable. Whereas the other. How need in the end? But how? How need in the end? (Beckett, 2006d, 454; Beckett, 1984b, 19).

Such a questioning of the basic need of the self and of the other is a questioning of the basic premises of the sovereign subject, especially since, as Anna McMullan describes it, there is a progressive and 'pervasive rejection or parody in Beckett's work of the concept of a sovereign, human, rational subject or agent who exercises control over the external environment through technology or *techné* (a will to make or create)' (McMullan, 2021, 7). Taking into consideration 'phallogocentrism' and its logics, it is no coincidence that such a radical questioning needs to take the figure of an aging woman in Beckett, not only because of the role of Beckett's own mother in his life and writing, but also because of the two logics functioning in modernism and modern thought according to Derrida: the logic of obsequence and the logic of pregnancy. As we have seen, both logics question the autonomy of the sovereign subject, especially as a male author who wants to re-create or re-make himself through his oeuvre, an act that carries with it the negation of his birth and mother. The logic of obsequence implies that the mother, like the old woman of *Ill Seen Ill Said* (but also of *Footfalls*, *Rockaby*, and the 'woman vanquished' in *The Lost Ones*), will not only have preceded him, but also will survive him. Such a precedence and survival are insinuated, in *Ill Seen Ill Said*, not only by the apparent ancient traits of the female figure, but also through the intimations of her identification with a clock or time itself. In its turn, as we have seen, the logic of pregnancy implies that anything written or expressed by the author, by his hand or his voice, would ultimately have always been contained within his mother, who, like the original surface or space of *khôra* or the primeval mud or *fango*, will always come both first and after him.[40]

---

[40] Even before the mud 'fango' had already appeared in Beckett's corpus through the Leopardi epigraph to Beckett's *Proust*: '*E fango è il mondo*' (the mud is the world).

The Sovereign's (an) Old Stancher

There is, at the beginning of the 2000 version of *Endgame*, directed by Conor McPherson, a curious sight. After a medium shot where Hamm yawns under the blood-stained handkerchief, there's a cut to a closer shot from behind his shoulder as he takes off the handkerchief and says his first line: 'Me ... to play'. Then we cut to this uncanny sight of his hands as he spreads and lays the old, widely stained handkerchief upon his crotch, saying the line 'Old stancher', while laying, carefully, almost caressingly his hands upon the blood-stained fabric. After this, we cut back to the shot over his shoulder, as he puts on his glasses, and then lifts the handkerchief in front of his face, just for a moment, in order to fold it and put it in his front pocket, while he coughs, and begins his first monologue.

While Claudia Olk is right in seeing the handkerchief both as 'a miniature version of the theatrical curtain' (Olk, 2022, 162) and a reminiscence of 'the magic garment that Prospero takes off at the beginning of *The Tempest* (*T.* 1.2 SD 24–5) and that he wears again at the end (*T* 5.1)' (162), McPherson's particular shot of Hamm's crotch underscores the uncanny bodily dimension of the sovereign that Beckett's play exposes. By putting the blood-stained handkerchief above Hamm's genitalia as he delivers the line 'Old stancher!' (Beckett, 2006c, 92) – which gets repeated at the end of the play, with Hamm's last words: 'Old stancher! / (Pause) / You ... remain' (154) – this version suggests not only Hamm's castration, but also that he – as the king and sovereign – is himself the 'old stancher'. In other words, there is a potential identification – through Beckett's common use of ellipsis – between him and the handkerchief ('Me ... to play [the] Old stancher'; 92]), which means that he is the 'one who, or that which stanches or stops a flow'. Thus, if as Anna McMullan has recently shown – following Martin Harries – *Endgame* can be seen as a play on the *theatrum mundi* tradition, it does so not only by questioning the existence of God (and his interests in humans) in this closed-off world, but also by examining the empty, castrated role of the sovereign in modernity, a role already analysed by Shakespeare and other authors, like Calderon de la Barca, within the tradition of the *theatrum mundi*.

In order to understand the role of the sovereign as an 'old stancher', let us briefly consider a painting realised at the moment of the ultimate crisis of sovereignty in France, right after the French Revolution of 1789: Jacques-Louis David's *The Death of Marat*. As Timothy J. Clark and Eric Santner have analysed it, this painting embodies the unstable historico-political moment when the French population did not know what to think not only about Marat, but also about the French Revolution at large. In it, above the revolutionary's dead body (represented androgynously, if not hermaphroditically, with a vulva-like wound reminiscent of mediaeval representations of Christ's own vagina-like cut on his side, and with a still erect pen in his hand), there is an empty space, covering almost half of the painting. If, as Santner explains, with this painting, the 'task was to put forth a body that would, as it were, incarnate the now empty place of the king, the figure that had traditionally been charged with corporeally representing the subject for all other subjects of the realm' (Santner, 2011, 92), the empty space above represents precisely the painting's failure at this task. In other words, it is the representation

> of nothing or nothing much – of an absence in which whatever the subject is has become present – but something more like a representation of painting, of painting as pure activity. Painting as material, therefore. Aimless. In the end detached from any one representational task. Bodily. (Clark qtd in Santner, 2011, 93)

Thus, the function of this empty upper half of the painting is reminiscent of the 'old stancher' as the empty place of the sovereign who is charged with 'stanching' or absorbing the bleeding flow of the subjects of all the realm, what Santner calls 'the flesh' (95). What is more, such an empty place of representation, or empty site of transcendence – the *Abgrund* or centre we saw before – appears doubled within *Endgame* in the picture, '*[h]anging near door, its face to wall*' (Beckett, 2006c, 91). However, as Olk remarks, perhaps this frame ultimately contains no referent, and it is not even a picture, given that it is 'turned against the wall as would be a mirror in the house of the deceased in Irish culture' (Olk, 2022, 159). Such an interpretation would make of that picture, like the 'old stancher' that Hamm holds '*spread out before him*' – as he says the words 'old stancher' – just another site of narcissistic reflection for the sovereign himself.

Hence, if the picture against the wall is not a painting but, like the blood-stained handkerchief, a mirror for the sovereign, it could contain all images, and significantly all sovereign subjects who – as in *Ghost Trio*'s screen framing the mirror for the spectators to see themselves – look into them. Furthermore, the constant possibility of an identification with the purportedly sovereign subject in Beckett's texts would make of most of his oeuvre, since the beginning – as Angela Moorjani remarked – a performative analysis and reflection of the subject as sovereign, as well as of the ongoing deconstruction of such an entity:

> The figures of the King, the sovereign author, the narcissistic artist, and the autonomous subject of rational philosophy all topple with *Murphy*. An old logocentric order explodes. [...] The undermining of the subject, which Freud announced and which the deconstructive criticism of the latter half of the twentieth century has been pursuing, is replayed by all of Beckett's texts from *Murphy* on. (Moorjani, 1982, 81)

As we have been showing, such a reflection on the constitutive narcissism of the male sovereign subject in its different instantiations (king, father, author, artist) connects Beckett's and Derrida's project, especially since the latter defined the aporias of narcissism as 'the explicit theme of deconstruction' (Derrida, 2006b, 122). Thus, it is not surprising that, just as Derrida's last seminar at the EHESS (*Ecole des Hautes Etudes en Sciences Sociales*) in 2001–3 was focused on 'The Beast and the Sovereign', Beckett studies have, in the past decades, focused more and more on his questioning of the male sovereign human, particularly regarding the non-human animal and the non-human world.

In the first volume of this last seminar – while commenting on a chapter of Louis Marin's book, *Le Portrait du roi*, focused on the project of a history of Louis XIV by his court historian, Pelisson – Derrida remarks how the representation of the king's history mimics the representation of Absolute Knowledge in Hegel:

> The point is to behave as though the spectacle, as it were, when read, were taking place from the point of view of absolute knowledge, as though the reader knew in advance what was going to happen, since everything is known in advance by the king. (Derrida, 2009, 288)

However, what interests Derrida the most is not so much this pre-supposed and pre-positioned sovereignty of the king guiding its (and his personal) pro-grammed history, but rather the transfer of such narrative sovereignty unto the reader. In other words, as Derrida sees it, by projecting a book from the ending and fulfilling point of sovereignty as absolute or kingly, the writer gives the reader, through 'this simulacrum-effect' (289), congenital to sovereignty, the chance to, as it were, borrow or even partake in this sovereignty, feeling thus themselves as absolute, fulfilled, and untouchable, as the ultimate sovereign:

> by giving the reading or watching subject of the narrative representation the illusion of himself pulling sovereignly the strings of history/the story or of the marionette, the mystification of representation is constituted by this simulac-rum of a true transfer of sovereignty. The reader, the spectator of this 'history of the king' has the illusion of knowing everything in advance, of sharing absolute knowledge with the king, and of *himself producing the story* that is being recounted to him. He participates in sovereignty, a sovereignty he shares or borrows. (Derrida, 2009, 289–90, my emphasis)

If such a simulacrum is an essential trait – 'congenital', says Derrida – of sovereignty, it is because the sovereign, in our tradition at least, is conceived, as Derrida shows, as the one who has the power to say and determine himself absolutely autarchic, that is to say, not only auto-regulated, but also auto-created.

Commenting, thus, on Aristotle's definition of the best nature of the best things in his *Politics*, Derrida says:

> That's the ontological definition of sovereignty, namely that it's better – since we're trying to live well (*eu zên*) – to live in autarchy, i.e. having in ourselves our principle, having in ourselves our commencement and our commande-ment, is better than the contrary. (Derrida, 2009, 345–6)

Such autarchy implies not only, as we have seen, a remaking of oneself that cancels birth and, consequently, maternity and the mother, but also an ultimate, absolute solitude, or the solitude of the absolute ruler. Examining the etymology of 'absolute' (Derrida, 2011, 1), exposes this essential solitude of the ultimate sovereign as its essential trait and condition of possibility. According to this logic, only an absolute sovereign can say 'I am alone', and it can only say it to himself: '"I am alone" does moreover mean "I am" absolute, that is absolved, detached or delivered from all bond, *absolutus*, safe from any bond, exceptional, even sover-eign'. In other words, 'The sovereign is alone (sovereign) or he is not' (8.).

While all of Beckett's oeuvre, and especially *Malone Dies* can be seen as a reflection on solitude and aloneness, the most engaged exploration of the paradoxes of sovereignty and solitude takes place in *Company*.[41] As we know, similarly to *How It Is*, this text explores acts of citation or dictation, whereupon the listening or repeating characters appear reflected and undecidably multiplied into a series. Beginning with a statement and a command that confuse Austin's distinction between a performative and a constative – bringing to mind Derrida's own analysis of this Austinian distinction in 'Signature Event Context' and *Limited Inc* – the text begins by, as it were, opening an echo without originary voice, at the same time that it gives the reader the impossible task to contain it: 'A voice comes to one in the dark. Imagine' (Beckett, 2006d, 427). The use of the second and third persons allows the text to multiply the listening and speaking (or writing) instances without ever stopping the reflection through the assumption of a responsible (in the sense of responsive) first person. Nevertheless, early on in the text, the possibility that all that is heard and said belongs to only one person is mentioned as a question, and given a potential answer underscoring the doubt and embarrassment of such a sovereign monologuing subject:

> If he is *alone* on his back in the dark why does the voice not say so? Why does it never say for example, You saw the light on such and such a day and now you are *alone* on your back in the dark? Why? Perhaps for no other reason than to kindle in his mind this faint uncertainty and embarrassment. (Beckett, 2006d, 428; my emphasis).

---

[41] While there is a similar exploration of aloneness in *Not I*, Mouth is not allowed a recognition of it at the end – or even complete aloneness – given the 'Auditor'.

Such a possibility, embodied by the term 'alone', will not come back until the end
of the text, when, after declaring the 'fable of one fabling with you in the dark'
(450) about to end, the last two lines of the text, separated as two paragraphs,
affirm the absolute aloneness of the sovereign speaker and reader: 'And you as
you always were. // Alone' (450). The affirmation of such a constative and
performative statement would, as we can expect, allow the listening/speaking
subject to finally utter the impossible first person, or as the text calls it, 'The
unthinkable last of all. Unnamable. Last person. I' (434). Thus, finally recognising and taking responsibility for all statements, this voice ends up being not only
the literal dictator of the whole text, but also its sovereign, since, as Derrida
remarks, 'dictatorship is always the essence of sovereignty' (Derrida, 2009, 67).
In other words, by finally acknowledging the absolute solitude of its absolute – as
detached and unbound from anyone else – state, and thus, by fulfilling the famous
command of the temple of Apollo at Delphi, 'know thyself', the speaking/
listening subject would recognise itself as the master, prince, or sovereign: 'The
master (and what is said of the master is easily transferable to the first of all, the
prince, the sovereign), the master is he who is said to be, and who can say
"himself" to be, the (self-)same, "myself"' (67).

If *Company* is written thus, finally, like the monarch's history of Pelisson,
namely,with a final recognition of the sovereign subject as he who was always
already at the end and at the beginning of his story, this final recognition is not
only that of the fictional first person, alone, 'I' character, but also that of its
reader. In other words, the text performs too 'this simulacrum of a true transfer
of sovereignty' (Derrida, 2009, 289) between its master, dictator, and sovereign,
and its reader, who cannot but identify with this absolute position, and thus, with
its absolute solitude. Yet, such an identification via transfer includes all the
tremors of its process, together with all the reflections and unstoppable multi-
plications within the text, namely: 'this faint uncertainty and embarrassment'
(Beckett, 2006d, 428) that stops the first person (singular or plural) from
recognising his absolute solitude, and thus, from saying I.[42] However, if, at
the end, the speaking/listening voices do recognise their voice in the final
adjective, 'alone', and if the reader responds, with them, to such an invocation,
by perhaps saying to themselves, 'yes, it is me, *alone*', such an act of response,
paradoxically, makes them both, character and reader, less sovereign than it
seems. This is because, if something defines the sovereign in its absolute
solitude and detachment from anyone and anything else, it is precisely his
absolute lack of responsibility. In other words, the sovereign is ultimately not

---

[42] As L. A. C. Dobrez expresses it: 'No identity at all remains. Solitude is now total, it is, as it were,
the solitude of no one' (qtd in Katz, 1999, no. 13, 207).

responsible because, as absolute sovereign, it does not have to respond of anything to anyone:[43]

> And that is indeed the most profound definition of absolute sovereignty, of the absolute of sovereignty, of the absoluteness that absolves it, unbinds it from all duty of reciprocity. The sovereign does not respond, he is the one who does not have to, who always has the right not to, respond [*répondre*], in particular not to be responsible for [*répondre de*] his acts. (Derrida, 2009, 57; Derrida 2008, 91).

If *Company* – like *How It Is*, *Endgame*, and a late text like *What Where* – examines and criticises precisely this lack of responsibility of the sovereign, it is because it shows not only the paradoxes of absolute sovereignty, but also the impossibility of its complete annulment. In this way, Beckett, like Derrida, exposes how, if there is not an opposite of sovereignty – a pantheist space without distinction – there is, nevertheless, always, as *Company* shows – in its dizzying multiplication of listeners/speakers – the possibility of a division, a fragmentation of the indivisibility purportedly essential to sovereignty. In other words, in works like *Company*, 'the question is not that of sovereignty or nonsovereignty but that of the modalities of transfer and division of a sovereignty said to be indivisible – said and supposed to be indivisible but always divisible' (Derrida, 2009, 291). As we know, such a division and sharing of sovereignty (*partage*) explains part of the difficulty of certain of Beckett's texts, as well as their abysmal character. This is the division and sharing that dictates the pseudo-sovereignty of the series Belacqua, Murphy, Watt, Mercier, Camier, Molloy, Moran, Malone, Macmann, Saposcat, Lemuel, Worm, Basil, Mahood, the Unnamable, Pim, Bam, Bem, Bim, Bom, and so on. If such a division is constantly threatening and hindering absolute sovereignty, it is due to the performative neotenic, *khôratic* surfaces of Beckett's texts, through which the characters, unborn, remain in a space of primary narcissism. This is also what makes the bottom or depths of Beckett's texts an abyss, as well as the temptation and haunting of stupidity mentioned by the unnamable ('Stupid obsession with depth'; Beckett, 2006b, 287; Beckett, 1992, 10). This haunting of *khôra*, the depths, the foundation (*Urgrund*), and the bottomless (*Ungrund*) abyss (*Abgrund*) that we inherited from German Idealism and Romanticism, is also their seduction, especially when we think that, like the sovereign subject, this abyss must be only one, and consequently, absolute. However, as these Beckettian series show, the

---

[43] Amanda Dennis hints at such an ultimate sovereign irresponsibility of Hamm, describing him as 'irresponsible in the sense of unresponsive to what was going on around him' (Dennis, 2021, 107).

centre or abyss looked for by his characters, and which they continuously avoid, is never truly one nor really alone:

> The abyss is not the bottom {*fond*}, the originary ground (*Urgrund*), of course, not the bottomless depth (*Ungrund*) of some hidden bottom or background {*fond*}. The abyss, if there is an abyss, is that there is *more than one* ground [*sol*], more than one solid, and more than one single threshold [*plus d'un seul seuil*]. More than one alone/no more one alone {*Plus d'un seul seul*}.
> That's where we are. (Derrida, 2009, 334; Derrida, 2008, 442; parentheses and brackets in original, {} mine)

Conclusion: Apostrophes and Addresses

As Katz expresses it: 'In Beckett, the "I" is not a representative of full subjectivity, but one marker within a subjective economy which necessarily comprises the second-person position, with its implicit demand' (1999, 107). In other words, Beckett's oeuvre, as well as Derrida's, is essentially an act of address. In different ways, they both reflect on Althusser's 'interpellation' as a 'double specular relation', exposing its aporias, particularly with regard to primary narcissism. Beckettian texts like *Company*, *That Time*, and even the early 'Sedendo et Quiescendo' with its opening line: 'Down you get now and step around' (Beckett, 2006d, 61), apostrophise us, the reader, directly, utilising the second person pronoun 'you'. Other texts present us with an almost direct address, marked either with irony, as when Clov, in *Endgame*, picking up the telescope and turning it '*on auditorium*', exclaims 'I see … a multitude … in transports … of joy' (Beckett, 2006c, 112), or with silent urgency and even effrontery, as when the Protagonist in *Catastrophe* '*raises his head, fixes the audience*' (489). One of the most particular acts of address or apostrophe happens, without words, in *Film*, where, by beginning and ending the work with an extreme close-up of Buster Keaton's eye, the film not only comments on its philosophical chase and anticipates the final deadly encounter between eye (E) and object (O), but also, and most importantly, identifies E/O with the spectators through this sight, making them both subject and object of this final vision. Such an identification through an optic direct address – which seems to visually state 'I/eye am you, the I/eye' – reflects as well other narcissistic identificatory encounters in Beckett's work, like those between Listener and Reader in *Ohio Impromptu*, May and Mother/Amy and old Mrs. Winter in *Footfalls*, or Molloy and Moran in *Molloy*.

As the resulting affect of any command of which we are the object tells us, such acts of direct address or apostrophe are always, in varying degrees, violent. This violence is particular in Beckett, since sometimes it involves a command to do a certain violence to our mental faculties like the imagination and discursive reason ('Imagination Dead Imagine', *Worstward Ho, How It Is*).[44] At other times, such direct addresses violently identify us with characters in emotional states like melancholy, nostalgia, and even guilt (*Company, Eh Joe, That Time*). At the same time, by performatively reflecting on this violence of the address and the identification, Beckett's texts problematise it, questioning the innocuity of a gesture as apparently simple as a couple looking at each other's eyes, as when Krapp narrates:

> I asked her to look at me and after a few moments – [*Pause.*] – after a few moments she did, but the eyes just slits, because of the glare. I bent over her to get them in the shadow and they opened. [*Pause. Low.*] Let me in. (Beckett, 2006c, 227)

Or when, at the end of *Happy Days*, Willie and Winnie look at each other, the latter first smiling, but then losing the smile, freezing in the potentially ominous long pause that ends the play.

In a text accompanying Marie-Françoise Plissart's photographic novel *Droit de regards*, where a series of couples have amorous encounters while they chase and run away from each other, Derrida examines the aporias of the direct visual address, by analysing the French pronominal verb '*se regarder*' (to look at each other, or at oneself), and how it applies to different instantiations between two people. Following the photographic examples in the text, he describes three possibilities of the sentence '*Elle se regardent*' (they look at each other). Furthermore, because he is also performatively reflecting on such a reflection by writing the text as a dialogue between two unnamed voices, he adds apostrophes to his description (for example, 'comme je t'aime' meaning potentially 'how [much] I love you').

1. *Elles se regardent*: One looks at the other, one looking at the other who doesn't *necessarily* look back at the moment she is seen. [. . .]
2. *Elles se regardent*: Each one looks at *herself* (*se regarde*) in a mirror, without seeing the other. [. . .]
3. *Elles se regardent*: Both look at each other, their gazes intersecting, as one says, being exchanged, watching the other watch her, right in her eyes, with infinite speculation [I see the other seeing me see her, I look at you at the instant you watch me watching you]. *Here you do not have a single example of that* – for, like 'I love you' [comme je t'aime], it cannot but escape the camera lens. Even if they cross their gazes in a face to face, like they *seem* to do once [. . .] the photography does not give us any assurance of it, the perception of it is impossible. (Derrida and Plissart, 1998, XXVII–XXVIII)

---

[44] Finney describes it as 'assault[ing] the foundations of verbal communication' (qtd in Dennis, 2021, 178).

Transposing these three instances to Beckett's work, we can say that number 1 is quite common, with characters like Clov exemplifying it the most with his apparent scopophilia. We have seen instances of number 2 in plays like *Ghost Trio*, and the speculative reflection is also at the base of Beckettian doppelgänger plays like *Ohio Impromptu*, *Footfalls*, and even in the lines of *Rockaby*, describing 'all eyes / all sides / high and low /for another / another like herself' (Beckett, 2006c, 462–3). Finally, number 3 describes Winnie and Willie at the end of *Happy Days*, as well as the lake anecdote told by Krapp. Nevertheless, its two most striking instantiations occur in *Murphy* and in *Film*. In the novel, it takes place close to the end, just a couple of pages before Murphy's own death. After their now infamous game of chess, 'Murphy [. . .] took Mr. Endon's head in his hands and brought the eyes to bear on his, or rather his on them, across a narrow gulf of air, the merest hand's-breath of air' (Beckett, 2006a, 149). Initially, Murphy sees the eyes as things, not as sight itself, with the novel itemising their 'sockets', 'the whites', 'iris', 'the red frill of mucus', and even 'the filigree of veins like the Lord's Prayer on a toenail' (149). Finally, he sees 'in the cornea, horribly reduced, obscured and distorted, his own image' (149).[45] Such a self-reflection (*se regarder*) provokes in Murphy a kind of synaesthesia, where the sight produces a voice and discourse, what the novel calls, playing with the different meanings of spirit as pneuma or gas (*Geist*), 'afflatulence' (150). Such spirit or gas describes not only the identification of Murphy's self in and with Mr. Endon's sight, but also its consequential disappearance, not as vanishment, but as a remarked erasure of sight, what Beckett calls 'unseen'.

> Murphy heard words demanding so strongly to be spoken that he spoke them, right into Mr. Endon's face, Murphy who did not speak at all in the ordinary way unless spoken to, and not always even then.
> 'the last at last seen of him
> himself unseen by him
> and of himself'.
> A rest.
> 'The last Mr. Murphy saw of Mr. Endon was Mr. Murphy unseen by Mr. Endon. This was also the last Murphy saw of Murphy'.
> A rest.
> 'The relation between Mr. Murphy and Mr. Endon could not have been better summed up than by the former's sorrow at seeing himself in the latter's immunity from seeing anything but himself'.
> A long rest.
> 'Mr. Murphy is a speck in Mr. Endon's unseen'. (Beckett, 2006a, 149–50)

---

[45] As Katz (1999, 154) remarks in *Dream*, there is an analogous attempt by Belacqua to see himself in the eyes of the Alba, yet this attempt is foiled by her closing her eyes.

In the case of *Film*, as we have seen, Beckett exemplifies Derrida's remark on the impossibility of the perception of such an act of mutual visual self-reflection through the loop of the extreme close-up of the singular eye at the beginning and end of the film. As we realise at the end, this loop embodies both eyes (*I*s), E's and O's, while at the same time, it 'swallows', in its gap or in between, the (I/eye of the) self-reflective spectator in it, making them identify with both seer I and seen (O). Thus, it is by the temptation to close this loop between the one-who-sees and the-one-who-is-seen (a loop that will infinitely invert these positions, identifying them [O=E, S=P, the being is what it perceives: *Esse est percipi*]), that the spectator will potentially embody, by responding with their total acquiescence (as we inevitably acquiesce to the identification with the 'you' of *Company* or *That Time*), a non-objectifying sight, that is, a potentially non-violent sight. In other words, in the purported total reciprocity of this looking at each other, both seer/seen and seen/seer would have the chance to avoid the violence of objectification, implicit in any relation between a subject and an object.

As we know, this is the kind of objectifying relation that Beckett diagnosed in the history of art in *Three Dialogues with Georges Duthuit*. If, ultimately, Beckett embraces the failure that he sees in Bram van Velde's painting as an ideal, namely, the failure of the absence of relation, such an absence does not deny the necessity of the relation nor its presupposed 'dualist view' (Beckett, 2006d, 562). In fact, such a failure or renunciation can only take place through the relation itself. In other words, Beckett's famous aesthetics of nonrelation imply an affirmation of the relation itself even if as impossible or always failed:

> if the occasion appears as an unstable term of relation, the artist, who is the other term, is hardly less so, thanks to his warren of modes and attitudes. The objections to this dualist view of the creative process are unconvincing. (562)

What is more, if the relation – even as absent or failed – is productive for Beckett, it is precisely through the particular kind of anxiety that it elicits.[46] This is not an anxiety of a missing adequation, as with a realistic, mimetic theory of representation or *adaequatio* vision of truth, but rather the anxiety of all that is excluded not only through a singular relation, but also in order that that singular relation can exist. In other words, it is the anxiety of the exclusionary singularity of any relation:

> All that should concern us is the acute and increasing anxiety of the relation itself, as though shadowed more and more darkly by a sense of invalidity, of inadequacy, of *existence at the expense of all that it excludes*, all that it blinds to. The history of painting, here we go again, is the history of its attempts to

---

[46] For a consideration of this Beckettian failed relation in comparison to Lacan's affirmation of the non-existence of sexual relation, see Chattopadhyay (2019).

escape from this sense of failure, by means of more authentic, more ample, *less exclusive relations between representer and representee*, in a kind of tropism towards a light as to the nature of which the best opinions continue to vary. (Beckett, 2006d, 562–3; my emphasis)

It is precisely this violence of exclusion that can never be avoided. Since, even if we have a potential reciprocal sight of subject and object, artist and model, E and O, and so on, such a sight can never be represented. It can never be shared, opened to a third eye, and thus confirmed. In fact, as Derrida says, it cannot even be confirmed by yourself if you are part of this reciprocal sight, since you are, too, seeing, and thus blind to the other's sight. Or, as Amanda Dennis expresses it in connection to Merleau-Ponty, 'we cannot be both subject and object at the same time' (Dennis, 2021, 181). To consider this aporia in terms of discursive address, we could say that, even if the fictional work addresses me directly with a 'you', I can never be sure that it is truly me. In a similar way, due to the underdetermined referent of the direct address, together with the repetition essential to language and discourse, when addressing 'you', I can also never be sure – like the characters in *How It Is*, *Company*, or the voice(s) of *The Unnamable* – that my words are truly mine, or that they are addressing the 'you' I intend.

Derrida examined such an aporia of the direct address in the context of his discussion with Lacan of Poe's 'The Purloined Letter' – and of the Lacanian idea that the letter (or truth) always arrives to its destination – in 'Envois'. As he does in *Memoirs of the Blind*, *Droit de regards*, and other texts, Derrida utilises here the French informal pronoun *tu*, not only as an imitation of the epistolary novel and philosophical dialogues, but also to underscore the aporias of the direct address, and its effects for both, fictional and philosophical discourse. In this way, he reinforces one of the main points of his whole oeuvre, the idea that philosophy, like literature, because it is a writing practice, cannot do without a writing subject, and more importantly, without a written addressee. Thus, for example, when speaking of a hypothetical postcard of Socrates, he asks:

Socrates' post card. To whom do you think he is writing? For me it is always more important to know that than to know what one is writing; moreover, I think it goes back to the same, to the other finally. (Derrida, 1987a, 21)

Thus if, in the question of this address of philosophy, there is an identification, or a confusion between the same and the other,[47] it is precisely – as in *Company* – because of the impossibility to determine who addresses whom: me – another,

---

[47] For Uhlmann, it is this inclusion of the other in the same that distinguishes Derrida's project from Levinas, and simultaneously approaches it to Beckett's oeuvre (Uhlmann, 1999, 167). This interior–exterior otherness is also what Daniel Katz sees as the coincidence between Joyce, Beckett, and Derrida (Katz, 1999, 151).

another – me, me – the other in me, the other in me – yet another in me, and so on, just as the diverse centres and circles in their search for each other or yet another in the painting in Erskine's room.

Therefore, like in *Company*, the question of such philosophical or written address for Derrida also spells the possibility of a solipsism, and of the kind of nihilism that, as we mentioned at the beginning, he saw both existing and not existing in Beckett's oeuvre, and in metaphysics at large. If such a nihilism can be the consequence of a solipsism, it is because, as with the conclusion of *Company*, there is always the possibility that, at the end, there is no addressee, just one voice alone, in delirium: 'or are we delirious, each alone, for ourselves? Are we waiting for an answer or something else? No, since at bottom [*au fond*] we are asking for nothing, no, we are asking no question. The prayer' (Derrida, 1987a, 19; Derrida, 1980, 24). This is why, perhaps, for a certain Beckett 'the prayer is the god. Yes, prayer rather than poem, in order to be quite clear, because poems are prayers, of Dives and Lazarus one flesh' (Beckett, 2009, 274). In other words, the poem or, rather, the poetic, is the only possibility of trans-cendence, in the sense that it is the only way to potentially cross the gap, the gulf, the chiasm[48] ($\chi\acute{\alpha}\sigma\mu\alpha$ $\mu\acute{\epsilon}\gamma\alpha$; Luke 16:26) of the relation – like Mr. Kelly and his kite at the end of *Murphy*;[49] or like a hedgehog trying to cross the road.

As Szafraniec (2007) and I (Martell, 2020) have pointed out, there is a poetic coincidence in Beckett and Derrida, in the figure of a hedgehog 'out in the cold' (Beckett, 2006d, 436). For Derrida, the poetic takes this figure because it is an attempt at transmission or translation, in other words, a trans-movement trying to connect (at least) two elements of a relation. However, the poetic is not any kind of communicational connection. Following the confusion of the direct address, it is a transmission whereupon the writer or speaker cannot determine anymore not only whom are they addressing, but also if their words are ultimately their own. Such an underdetermination, for Derrida, means that the poetic not only can confuse the interior and the exterior sources of the words, as a dictation. What is more radical is that it can confuse them so essentially that, that which we deem our utmost interior, the 'heart', is precisely what the poetic teaches us, as if we did not have a heart before. As Derrida expresses it, 'You did not yet know the heart, you learn it thus' (Derrida, 1991, 231). In other words, if, as Beckett described it, the poem is the prayer and the god, it is because the poetic is that particular chance to find the most personal expression, one's own idiom, but always from outside – or *auswendig*, as Derrida remarks, emphasising that that is how one says 'by heart' in German, literally 'turning from the outside'.

---

[48] For a reading of Merleau-Ponty's notion of chiasm vis-à-vis Beckett, see Dennis (2021)

[49] It is precisely the mention of Mr. Kelly and his kite as a poem that introduces, in the letter to McGreevy, the idea of the poem as prayer (Beckett, 2009, 274).

Now, such a chance – like the hedgehog that the voice in *Company* tells 'you take pity on' and 'put it in an old hatbox with some worms' (Beckett, 2006d, 436) (or, in French 'avec une provision de vers' (Beckett, 2004a, 38), which might be translated as 'with a provision of verses') – can always turn awry, and the hedgehog, as one of the main figures of modernism, might die and rot, even if it always remains in your memory:[50] 'You have never forgotten what you found then [. . .] The mush. The stench' (437). For Derrida, it is the possibility of such a survival through repetition that ultimately might mean death, since learning 'by heart' also means learning 'by rote', namely mechanically, auto-matically, 'soullessly', 'not-lively', and perhaps, 'not-livingly', since, as the young Beckett who wrote *Proust* would say: 'Memory and Habit are attributes of the Time cancer' (Beckett, 2006d, 515).[51] Consequently, the chance for the poetic to live is to remain as an absolute secret, pronounced only one time, and then protected and covered by oblivion, even and especially in the confusion of the address(e)es and the words' origins:

> You give me the words, you deliver them, dispensed one by one, my own, while turning them towards yourself and addressing them to yourself – and I have never loved them so, the most common ones become quite rare, nor so loved to lose them either, to destroy them by forgetting at the very instant when you received them, and this instant would precede almost everything, my *envoi*, myself, destroying them in oblivion, before me, so that they take place only once. One single time, you see how crazy this is for a word? Or for any trait at all? (Derrida, 1987a, 12; Derrida 1980, 17).

This is the double bind of the repetition necessary for poetry, literature, philoso-phy, and writing at large to exist. While it is such a repetition that kills its singular character, its idiomaticity, and the sovereignty of both addresser and addressee. This is the double bind of texts like *How It Is*, and their failed attempts at finishing in order to stop repeating. It is the same double bind of the Beckettian circles, unable to stop the repetition but also to fully complete it, expressed in the 'and yet' of *Endgame*'s 'The end is in the beginning and yet you go on' (Beckett, 2006c, 141). But most importantly, it is the double bind of the necessary repetition inherent to any address to the other. This is the necessary repetition of the reflective Narcissus, be it in the form of a bent-over-himself

---

[50] As his mention of Jules Renard's hedgehog in a letter to MacGreevy shows (Beckett, 2009, 252), Beckett knew the symbolic significance of the hedgehog for modernism and Romanticism, including potentially Friedrich Schlegel's famous description of the fragment as a hedgehog.

[51] Examining the conception of time in Beckett as Steven J. Rosen develops it in *Samuel Beckett and the Pessimistic Tradition*, and comparing it with Derrida's analysis of Hamlet's line 'the time is out joint', Uhlmann comments: 'Reading Rosen through Derrida, the point might be made in passing that it could be possible to identify Beckett's concept of "habit" with the notion of injustice Derrida is developing here' (Uhlmann, 1999, 178, n. 23).

Belacqua, a Molloy reflected in a Moran, or a Samuel Beckett reflected in all the series of characters of his oeuvre, including the female and queer ones. This is the double bind of the writer trying to address somebody else besides themselves, either as readers, love objects, or both, but incapable of doing so without repeating and reflecting themselves in an inescapable and resurgent primary narcissism (see Freud, 1957). If Derrida and Beckett shared the insight of this double bind, it is because they recognised its aporetic necessity, together with the need to rethink narcissism, in writing, until there is (no) more of it:

> One can only love oneself. One will have understood nothing of the love of the other, of you, of the other as such, you understand/hear, without a new intelligence of narcissism, a new 'patience', a new passion for narcissism. The right to narcissism must be rehabilitated, it needs the time and the means. (No) more narcissism. Always (no) more narcissism – well comprehended, comprising that of the other. (Derrida and Plissart, 2010, XXVIII).

Finally, as we know, such a problematisation of primary narcissism is, in some way, the plot of *The Unnamable*, *Texts for Nothing*, and other fictions. In other words, it is the reason why these 'characters' are simultaneously always already dead and not yet born, undistinguishable from the surrounding and internal other that comprehends them, inside out, in this suspension of individualising birth, our sojourn in *khôra*.

Bibliography

Abbot, H. Porter (1996), *Beckett Writing Beckett: The Author in the Autograph*, Cornell: Cornell University Press.

Ackerley, Chris J. (2006), 'An "Other Object of Note": Circle and Point in Samuel Beckett's *Watt*', *Samuel Beckett Today / Aujourd'hui*, 16, pp. 319–32.

Bailey, Helen and William Davies, eds (2021), *Beckett and Politics*, Cham: Palgrave.

Bair, Deirdre (1978), *Samuel Beckett*, New York: Summit Books.

Beckett, Samuel (1958), *Nouvelles et textes pour rien*, Paris: Les éditions de minuit.

Beckett, Samuel (1969), *Comment c'est*, Paris: Les éditions de minuit.

Beckett, Samuel (1984a), *Disjecta, Miscellaneous Writings and a Dramatic Fragment*, ed. Ruby Cohn, New York: Grove Press.

Beckett, Samuel (1984b), *Mal vu mal dit*, Paris: Les éditions de minuit.

Beckett, Samuel (1989), *Molloy*, Paris: Les éditions de minuit.

Beckett, Samuel (1992), *L'innommable*, Paris: Les éditions de minuit.

Beckett, Samuel (2000), *Obra poética completa*, Madrid: Hiperión.

Beckett, Samuel (2001), *Fin de partie*, Paris: Les éditions de minuit.

Beckett, Samuel (2004a), *Compagnie*, Paris: Les éditions de minuit.

Beckett, Samuel (2004b), *Malone meurt*, Paris: Les éditions de minuit.

Beckett, Samuel (2006a), *The Grove Centenary Edition. Volume I: Novels*, ed. Paul Auster, New York: Grove Press.

Beckett, Samuel (2006b), *The Grove Centenary Edition. Volume II: Novels*, ed. Paul Auster, New York: Grove Press.

Beckett, Samuel (2006c), *The Grove Centenary Edition. Volume III: Dramatic Works*, ed. Paul Auster, New York: Grove Press.

Beckett, Samuel (2006d), *The Grove Centenary Edition. Volume IV: Poems, Short Fiction, and Criticism*, ed. Paul Auster, New York: Grove Press.

Beckett, Samuel (2009), *The Letters of Samuel Beckett, Vol. I: 1929–1940*, ed. Martha Dow Fehsenfeld and Lois More Overbeck, New York: Cambridge University Press.

Beckett, Samuel (2011), *The Letters of Samuel Beckett, Vol. II: 1941–1956*, ed. George Craig, Martha Dow Fehsenfeld, Dan Gunn, and Lois More Overbeck, New York: Cambridge University Press.

Beckett, Samuel (2016), *The Letters of Samuel Beckett, Vol. IV: 1966–1989*, ed. George Craig, Martha Dow Fehsenfeld, Dan Gunn, and Lois More Overbeck, New York: Cambridge University Press.

Beckett, Samuel (2020), *Samuel Beckett's Philosophy Notes*, ed. Steven Matthews and Matthew Feldman, Oxford: Oxford University Press.

Begam, Richard (1996), *Samuel Beckett and the End of Modernity*, Stanford: Stanford University Press.

Blanchot, Maurice (1978), *Death Sentence*, trans. Lydia Davis, Barrytown: Station Hill.

Boulter, Jonathan (2020), *Posthuman Space in Samuel Beckett's Short Prose*, Edinburgh: Edinburgh University Press.

Byron, Mark (2020), *Samuel Beckett's Geological Imagination*, Cambridge: Cambridge University Press.

Caselli, Daniela (2005), *Beckett's Dantes*, Manchester: Manchester University Press.

Caselli, Daniela (2023), *Insufferable: Beckett, Gender and Sexuality*. Cambridge: Cambridge University Press.

Chattopadhyay, Arka (2018), *Beckett, Lacan and the Mathematical Writing of the Real*, London: Bloomsbury.

Clément, Bruno (2009), *L'Œuvre sans qualités. Rhétorique de Samuel Beckett*, Paris: Seuil.

Coetzee, J. M. (2006), 'Introduction', in Samuel Beckett, *The Grove Centenary Edition. Volume IV*, New York: Grove Press, pp. ix–xiv.

Connor, Steven (2007), *Samuel Beckett: Repetition, Theory and Text*, Aurora: The Davies Group.

Cordingley, Anthony (2018), *How It Is: Philosophy in Translation*, Edinburgh: Edinburgh University Press.

Deleuze, Gilles (1976), *Différence et répétition*, Paris: Presses universitaires de France.

Dennis, Amanda (2019), 'Samuel Beckett et la langue maternelle. Ambivalence et expatriation linguistique', in Yann Mével (ed.), *Samuel Beckett et la culture française*, Paris: Garnier, pp. 95–114.

Dennis, Amanda (2021), *Beckett and Embodiment: Body, Space, Agency*, Edinburgh: Edinburgh University Press.

Derrida, Jacques (1962), 'Introduction à l'origine de la géométrie de Husserl', in Edmund Husserl, *L'origine de la géométrie*, trans. Jacques Derrida, Paris: Presses universitaires de France, pp. 3–171.

Derrida, Jacques (1974), *Glas*, Paris: Galilée.

Derrida, Jacques (1978), *Writing and Difference*, trans. Alan Bass, Chicago: University of Chicago Press.

Derrida, Jacques (1979a), *L'écriture et la différence*, Manchecourt: Éditions du seuil.

Derrida, Jacques (1979b), *Marges de la philosophie*, Paris: Les éditions de minuit.

Derrida, Jacques (1980), *La carte postale*, Paris: Flammarion.

Derrida, Jacques (1982), *Margins of Philosophy*, trans. Alan Bass, Chicago: University of Chicago Press.

Derrida, Jacques (1984), *Edmund Husserl's 'Origin of Geometry': An Introduction*, trans. John P. Leavey Jr, Lincoln: University of Nebraska Press.

Derrida, Jacques (1986), *Parages*, Paris: Galilée.

Derrida, Jacques (1987a), *The Post Card*, trans. Alan Bass, Chicago: University of Chicago Press.

Derrida, Jacques (1987b), *Ulysse gramophone, Deux mots pour Joyce*, Paris: Galilée.

Derrida, Jacques (1991), *A Derrida Reader: Between the Blinds*, ed. Peggy Kamuf, New York: Columbia University Press.

Derrida, Jacques (1992), *Acts of Literature*, ed. Derek Attridge, New York: Routledge.

Derrida, Jacques (1993a), *Khôra*, Paris: Galilée.

Derrida, Jacques (1993b), *Memoirs of the Blind: The Self-Portrait and Other Ruins*, trans. Pascale-Anne Brault and Michael Naas, Chicago: University of Chicago Press.

Derrida, Jacques (1993c), *Spectres de Marx. L'état de la dette, le travail de deuil et la nouvelle Internationale*, Paris: Galilée.

Derrida, Jacques (1994), *Politiques de l'amitié*, Paris: Galilée.

Derrida, Jacques (1995), 'Khôra', in Jacques Derrida, *On the Name*, ed. Thomas Dutoit, Stanford: Stanford University Press, pp. 89–127.

Derrida, Jacques (1996), *Le monolinguisme de l'autre*, Paris: Galilée.

Derrida, Jacques (1998), *Monolingualism of the Other*, Stanford: Stanford University Press.

Derrida, Jacques (2000), *Etats d'âme de la psychanalyse*, Paris: Galilée.

Derrida, Jacques (2001), 'La veilleuse', in Jacques Trilling, *James Joyce ou l'écriture matricide*, Belfort: Circé, pp. 7–32.

Derrida, Jacques (2003), *Voyous. Deux essais sur la raison*, Paris: Galilée.

Derrida, Jacques (2004), 'Living On'/'Borderlines', in Harold Bloom, Paul de Man, Jacques Derrida, Geoffrey Hartman, and J. Hillis Miller, *Deconstruction and Criticism*, New York: Continuum, pp. 75–176.

Derrida, Jacques (2005a), *The Politics of Friendship*, trans. Georges Collins, London: Verso.

Derrida, Jacques (2005b), *Rogues. Two Essays on Reason*, trans. Pascale-Anne Brault and Michael Naas, Stanford: Stanford University Press.

Derrida, Jacques (2006a), 'Comment ne pas trembler?' *Annali della Fondazione europea del disegno*, Milan: Mondadori, pp. 91–103.

Derrida, Jacques (2006b), *Specters of Marx*, trans. Peggy Kamuf, New York: Routledge.

Derrida, Jacques (2007), *Learning to Live Finally*, trans. Pascale-Anne Brault and Michael Naas, New York: Palgrave.

Derrida, Jacques (2008), *La bête et le souverain I*, Paris: Galilée.

Derrida, Jacques (2009), *The Beast and the Sovereign. Volume I*, trans. Geoffrey Bennington, Chicago: University of Chicago Press.

Derrida, Jacques (2011), *The Beast and the Sovereign. Volume II*, trans. Geoffrey Bennington, Chicago: University of Chicago Press.

Derrida, Jacques (2012), 'La mélancholie d'Abraham', *Les Temps modernes*, 669–70, pp. 30–66.

Derrida, Jacques (2013), 'The Night Watch', 'Two Words for Joyce', 'Ulysses Gramophone', in Andrew J. Mitchell and Sam Slote (eds.), *Derrida and Joyce*, Albany: SUNY Press, pp. 87–108, 281–98, 41–86.

Derrida, Jacques (2021), *Clang*, trans. G. Bennington and David Wills, Minneapolis: University of Minnesota Press.

Derrida, Jacques and Derek Attridge (2009), 'Cette étrange institution qu'on appelle littérature', in Thomas Dutoit and Philippe Romanski (eds), *Derrida d'ici, Derrida de là*, Paris: Galilée, pp. 253–92.

Derrida, Jacques and Geoffrey Bennington (1991), *Jacques Derrida*, Tours: Seuil.

Derrida, Jacques and Geoffrey Bennington (1993), *Jacques Derrida*, trans. Geoffrey Bennington, Chicago: University of Chicago Press.

Derrida, Jacques and Michael Ben-Naftali (2017), 'Abraham's Melancholy', *Oxford Literary Review*, 39:2, pp. 153–88.

Derrida, Jacques and Marie-Françoise Plissart (1998), *Right of Inspection*, trans. David Wills, New York: Monacelli Press.

Derrida, Jacques and Marie-Françoise Plissart (2010), *Droit de regards*, Brussels: Les impressionnes nouvelles.

Dick, Kirby, and Amy Z. Kofman (2001), *Derrida: Screenplay and Essays on the Film*, New York: Routledge.

Dick, Kirby, and Amy Z. Kofman (2005), Derrida, New York: Routledge.

Feldman, Matthew (2006), *Beckett's Books*, New York: Continuum.

Freud, Sigmund (1946), *Gesammelte Werke. Schriften Aus dem Nachlass 1892–1938*, London: Imago.

Freud, Sigmund (1957), 'On Narcissism', in *The Standard Edition of the Complete Psychological Works of Sigmund Freud, Volume XIV (1914–1916)*, London: Hogarth Press, pp. 67–102.

Gontarski, S. E. (1996), 'Introduction', in Samuel Beckett, *Nohow On*, New York: Grove Press, pp. vii–xxviii.

Graham, Alan (2021), '"Made of Words": Beckett and The Politics of Language', in Helen Bailey and William Davies (eds), *Beckett and Politics*, Cham: Palgrave, pp. 55–68.

Hägglund, Martin (2008), *Radical Atheism*, Stanford: Stanford University Press.

Hegel, G. W. F. [1807] (1977), *Phenomenology of Spirit*, trans. A. V. Miller, New York: Oxford University Press.

Hegel, G. W. F. [1807] (2010), *Phänomenologie des Geistes*, Cologne: Anaconda.

Heidegger, Martin (2008), *Being and Time*, trans. John Macquarrie and Edward Robinson, New York: Harper.

Hiebel, Hans (1995), 'Quadrat 1 and 2 as a Television Play', *Samuel Beckett Today / Aujourd'hui*, 4, pp. 335–43.

Katz, Daniel (1999), *Saying I No More: Subjectivity and Consciousness in the Prose of Samuel Beckett*. Evanston, IL: Northwestern University Press.

Kearney, Richard (1995), *States of Mind*, New York: New York University Press.

Kenny, Eva (2020), 'A Fetish for Failure', *Dublin Review of Books*, https://drb .ie/articles/a-fetish-for-failure.

Knowlson, James (1996), *Damned to Fame: The Life of Samuel Beckett*, New York: Simon & Schuster.

Little, James (2020), *Samuel Beckett in Confinement: The Politics of Closed Space*, London: Bloomsbury.

Martell, James (2013), 'Between Beckett and Derrida: A Hegelian Death', in Arka Chattopadhyay and James Martell (eds), *Samuel Beckett and the Encounter of Philosophy and Literature*, London: Roman, pp. 136–55.

Martell, James (2020), 'How to Tremble beyond Sovereignty: Derrida's Beckettian Spectre', *Oximora*, 17, pp. 99–118.

Martell, James (2024a), 'Between the Ocean and the Ground: Giving Surfaces', *Derrida Today*, 17:1.

Martell, James (2024b), 'Modernism's Totalities: From the Marquis de Sade to Titus-Carmel', *Journal of Modern Literature*, 48:1.

Maude, Ulrika (2011), *Beckett, Technology, and the Body*, Cambridge: Cambridge University Press.

McMullan, Anna (2021), *Beckett's Intermedial Ecosystems*, Cambridge: Cambridge University Press.

Moorjani, Angela (1982), *Abysmal Games in the Novels of Samuel Beckett*, Chapel Hill: University of North Carolina Press.

O'Connell, Brenda (2021), 'Insufferable Maternity and Motherhood in "First Love"', in Helen Bailey and William Davies (eds), *Beckett and Politics*, Cham: Palgrave, pp. 107–21.

Olk, Claudia (2022), *Shakespeare and Beckett*, Cambridge: Cambridge University Press.

Plato (1903), *Platonis Opera*, ed. John Burnet, Oxford: Oxford University Press. www.perseus.tufts.edu/hopper/text?doc=Perseus%3Atext% 3A1999.01.0180%3Atext%3DTim.%3Asection%3D52a.

Rabaté, Jean-Michel (2016), *Think Pig! Beckett at the Limits of the Human*, New York: Fordham University Press.

Rabaté, Jean-Michel (2020), *Beckett and Sade*, Cambridge: Cambridge University Press.

Salisbury, Laura (2015), *Samuel Beckett: Laughing Matters, Comic Timing*, Edinburgh: Edinburgh University Press.

Santner, Eric (2011), *The Royal Remains*, Chicago: University of Chicago Press.

Schelling, F. W. J [1809] (2006), *Philosophical Investigations into the Essence of Human Freedom*, trans. Jeff Love and Johannes, Schmidt: SUNY Press.

Schulz, Hans-Joachim (1973), *This Hell of Stories: A Hegelian Approach to the Novels of Samuel Beckett*, The Hague: Mouton.

Sharkey, Rodney (2010), 'Beaufret, Beckett, and Heidegger: The Question of Influence', *Samuel Beckett Today / Aujourd'hui*, 22, pp. 409–22.

Simpson, Hannah (2022a), *Samuel Beckett and Disability Performance*, Cham: Palgrave.

Simpson, Hannah (2022b), *Samuel Beckett and the Theatre of the Witness*, Oxford: Oxford University Press.

Szafraniec, Asja (2007), *Beckett, Derrida, and the Event of Literature*, Stanford: Stanford University Press.

Trezise, Thomas (1990), *Into the Breach. Samuel Beckett and the Ends of Literature*, Princeton: Princeton University Press.

Uhlmann, Anthony (1999), *Beckett and Poststructuralism*, New York: Cambridge University Press.

Van Hulle, Dirk and Shane Weller (2014), *The Making of Samuel Beckett's* L'Innommable / The Unnamable, London: Bloomsbury.

Weller, Shane (2005), *A Taste for the Negative: Beckett and Nihilism*, London: Legenda.

Cambridge Elements ☰

Beckett Studies

Dirk Van Hulle
University of Oxford
Dirk Van Hulle is Professor of Bibliography and Modern Book History at the
University of Oxford and director of the Centre for Manuscript Genetics
at the University of Antwerp.

Mark Nixon
University of Reading
Mark Nixon is Associate Professor in Modern Literature at the University of Reading
and the Co-Director of the Beckett International Foundation.

About the Series

This series presents cutting-edge research by distinguished and emerging scholars,
providing space for the most relevant debates informing Beckett studies as well as
neglected aspects of his work. In times of technological development, religious
radicalism, unprecedented migration, gender fluidity, environmental and social crisis,
Beckett's works find increased resonance. Cambridge Elements in Beckett Studies is
a key resource for readers interested in the current state of the field.

Cambridge Elements ≡

Beckett Studies

Elements in the Series

Printed in the United States
by Baker & Taylor Publisher Services